RIVERS IN WORLD HISTORY

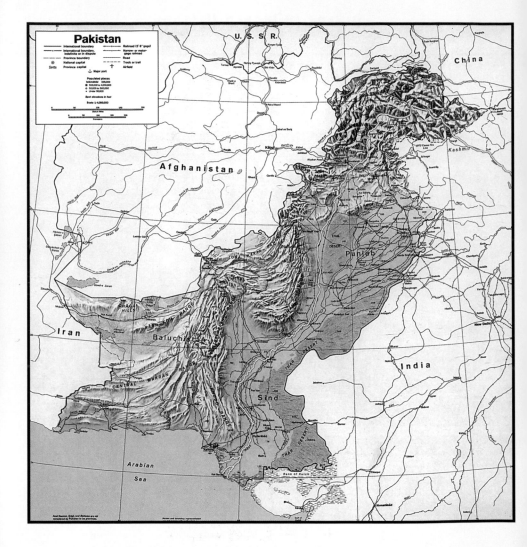

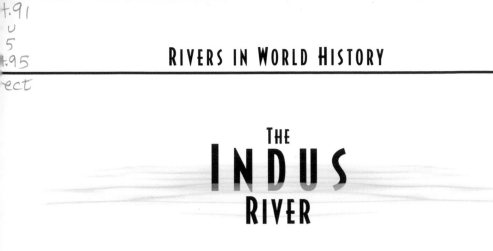

THE
INDUS
RIVER

Shane Mountjoy

Series Consulting Editor
Tim McNeese

CHELSEA HOUSE
PUBLISHERS
A Haights Cross Communications Company
Philadelphia

FRONTIS: The Indus River (highlighted in yellow) originates in the northern Himalaya Mountains, near Lake Mansarovar in Tibet, and flows 1,800 miles through Pakistan to the Arabian Sea.

CHELSEA HOUSE PUBLISHERS

VP, NEW PRODUCT DEVELOPMENT Sally Cheney
DIRECTOR OF PRODUCTION Kim Shinners
CREATIVE MANAGER Takeshi Takahashi
MANUFACTURING MANAGER Diann Grasse

Staff for THE INDUS RIVER

EXECUTIVE EDITOR Lee Marcott
EDITOR Christian Green
PRODUCTION EDITOR Noelle Nardone
PHOTO EDITOR Sarah Bloom
SERIES AND COVER DESIGNER Keith Trego
LAYOUT 21st Century Publishing and Communications, Inc.

A Haights Cross Communications ⬥ Company

First Printing

9 8 7 6 5 4 3 2 1

Library of Congress Cataloging-in-Publication Data

Mountjoy, Shane, 1967–
    The Indus River/Shane Mountjoy
        p. cm.—(Rivers in world history ; 1)
    Includes bibliographical references and index.
    ISBN 0-7910-8243-1
    1. Indus River Valley—Civilization. 2. Indus River Valley—Social life and customs. I. Title. II. Series.
DS423.M66 2005
954.91—dc22

                                                           2004018215

All links and Web addresses were checked and verified to be correct at the time of publication. Because of the dynamic nature of the Web, some addresses and links may have changed since publication and may no longer be valid.

CONTENTS

1

The Indus River and Valley

As it flows through Pakistan, the Indus River's unhurried waters pass through a region that is home to distinct religions and diverse cultures. From ancient times, the Indus has acted as the boundary between India and the rest of the world. Throughout history, it has served as the line of demarcation of the Middle East and Asia, separating that which is India and Indian from that which is Arab or Persian. When Alexander the Great led his troops across this great Indian river, he noticed that cultural traits such as clothing, food, language, and religion no longer resembled those of the Hellenistic or Persian territories. Babur, who in the sixteenth century established the Mogul Empire in northern India, made similar observations. He noted that, despite the rich diversity of peoples and customs throughout India, once one crossed the Indus heading south or east, "everything is in the Hindustan way; land, water, tree, rock, people and horde, opinion and custom." [1]

India has seemed to invite invaders throughout its history, in part because of its uniqueness and in part because of "the softness and effeminacy induced by the climate, and yielding nature of the soil, which produces almost spontaneously," often offering the natives up as "an easy prey to every foreign invader." [2] Thus, India's history includes numerous conquests, as one invading force after another, lured by resources and grandeur, entered the region and occupied the subcontinent. With each invasion came a fusion of the existing people and culture with the invading people and culture. The result was and is a richly diverse, exotic, and multifaceted Indian culture. According to twentieth-century anthropologist J.H. Hutton: "The subcontinent of India has been likened to a deep net into which various races and peoples of India have drifted and been caught." [3] As such, it is impossible to describe India or the history of the Indus in brief terms. Instead, for a portrayal to be adequate, one must examine many layers and include many different cultures to view "not one but many Indias." [4] The history of the Indus River, like that of the Indian subcontinent, is the story of many different influences that have entered the region and persisted over time.

INDIA'S DIVERSITY

Throughout the Indus' history, several different cultures have engaged in a struggle for supremacy and survival. These various races, languages, and religions have acted to divide the populace, not bring it together. Dozens of major languages and numerous dialects within each language have heightened the differences among these ethnicities. It does not help that not one, but many classical languages—including Dravidian, Old Iranian, Pali, Prakrit, and Sanskrit—make up India's literary tradition. More modern languages such as Arabic, English, and Persian also play a part in India's literary heritage.

Like language, religion in India is extremely diverse. Some people believe in animism, but India also claims adherents to Buddhism, Christianity, Islam, Jainism, Sikhism, Zoroastrianism, and Hinduism. Hinduism is the largest of India's religions, but it is itself a diverse religion with competing theologies and practices, often differing from village to village.

THE INDUS' INFLUENCE

Given the diverse makeup of India and its cultural characteristics, an obvious question emerges: How can there be any permanence to such a diverse culture that includes a number of castes, including the Brahmans (priests)? One scholar, D.D. Kosambi, wrote:

> India shows extraordinary continuity of culture. The violent breaks known to have occurred in the political and theological superstructure have not prevented long survivals of observances that have no sanction in the official Brahmin works, hence can only have originated in the most primitive stages of

human society; moreover, the Hindu scriptures, even more the observances sanctified in practice by Brahmanism, show adoption of non-Brahmin local rites. That is, the process of assimilation was mutual, a peculiar characteristic of India.[5]

Thus, the melding or at least the cohabitation of cultural traits with what we now describe as Indian culture was a long-term process that took place at the local level and included the incorporation of various traditions.

What is it then that helps bridge the differences among all of these peoples? In some respects, it is the Indus River. The Indus is one of the few constants in a place that has seen many changes over the centuries. The river acts as one of the few unifying features in the region: All who live there need the life-giving waters it carries. The importance of the river is one explanation for countless invasions into the region: The river sustains life for whomever lives there. This one unifying trait has ensured that the region will be filled with dissimilar people. These dissimilar peoples, with their various languages and competing religions, have sought to establish functioning societies on the Indus Plain and throughout India.

British cartographer James Rennell (1742–1830) once wrote that "India has in all ages excited the attention of the curious, in almost every walk of life."[6] This is no less true today. Today, the landmass we call the Indian subcontinent includes the countries of India, Pakistan, Nepal, Bangladesh, and Sri Lanka. This subcontinent is every bit as large as Western Europe and extends away from the cold and forbidding Himalaya Mountains into the warm and inviting Indian Ocean.

THE INDIAN SUBCONTINENT

The Indian subcontinent is a triangular landmass that juts out into the Indian Ocean. The Himalayas lie to the north and east, separating India from the rest of Asia. Lesser mountain ranges

The Indus River's delta forms just to the southeast of the world's sixteenth-largest city, Karachi, Pakistan, and flows into the Arabian Sea (shown here in a satellite image). The river's delta is recognized by conservationists as one of the world's most important ecological regions.

(the Kirthar and Sulaiman) and the Thar Desert help provide a buffer to the north and west. Three great rivers flank the northern boundaries of the subcontinent: The Indus waters the north-west and the Brahmaputra (which leads into the Ganges) and the Ganges water the northeast. The climate of the Indus basin varies. In the north are mountainous highlands and an alpine climate. On the plains in the provinces of Sindh and Punjab, one finds temperate subhumid conditions, semiarid lands, and even subtropical arid climates.

The Himalayas—the word means "house of snow" in Sanskrit —serve as the backdrop to the Indus River, and the melting snow from them becomes the waters of the Indus and Ganges Rivers. The mountains themselves stretch 1,500 miles in three parallel ranges that separate India from Tibet. These ranges are home to the world's youngest—but tallest—mountains. Forty of the 146 Himalayan peaks rise more than 25,000 feet. The runoff waters that create the Brahmaputra, Ganges, and Indus Rivers give life to the countryside; one of the most densely populated places on Earth. This region is known as the Indo-Gangetic Plain.

After being fed by the Brahmaputra, the Ganges empties into the Bay of Bengal by flowing southeast—but only after creating one of the largest delta plains in the world. This fertile land, located in Bangladesh and West Bengal, is home to many who rely on the waters of the river to raise crops. The Indus, which enters the Arabian Sea in the west, is the water source for some of the most fertile farmland in the world.

GEOGRAPHY OF THE INDUS RIVER

The Indus River can hardly be called the world's most important river, but it shares the distinction of being the most important river of the Indian subcontinent with the Ganges. Because the river passes through semiarid land, however, its importance to the regional population cannot be overstated. Its length measures 1,800 miles, and its annual flow is double that of the Nile, measuring 272 billion cubic yards.

The Indus River cannot even be termed the holiest of rivers on the Indian subcontinent: The Ganges claims that honor. Yet it is a river that tells many tales. The Indus River has served as a border, a vital source of agricultural irrigation, and the stage on which a diverse group of peoples, languages, and religions have gathered for more than 4,000 years. Without the Indus, the chronicles of India's history would be very different and less enchanting. Instead, the country's history might read as a dull narrative of a people living and dying in a harsh climate surrounded by rugged mountains and unforgiving arid lands.

Early Tibetans believed that the river originated from Lake Mansarovar, located in Tibet. Expeditions in the area later revealed that the Indus traces its source to just north of the lake. There are four rivers (the Brahmaputra, the Ganga or Ganges, the Karnali, and the Indus) that originate in this region. Symbolically, the four rivers were portrayed as coming out of different animals' mouths as a way to attribute different qualities to each of the rivers. The Brahmaputra is said to come from a horse's mouth, the Ganges from the mouth of an elephant, the Karnali from a peacock's mouth, and the Indus from the mouth of a lion. "The waters of the river Brahmaputra are cold and it is said that the one who drinks these waters would become sturdy as a horse."[7] Likewise, the Ganges is reputed to offer the admirable traits of an elephant: "good memory, sense of gratitude, strong, and auspicious."[8] The Karnali is said to offer the elegant beauty of a peacock. Finally, the Indus, which is warm, offers those who drink from it the courage and heroism of a lion.

Unquestionably, the source of the Indus is in Tibet. The river begins at the confluence of the Sengge and Gar Rivers, which drain the Nganglong Kangri and Gangdise Shan Mountains. From here, the river flows northwest, where it passes through Kashmir south of the Karakoram Mountains and then progressively turns southward, emerging from the hills between the Pakistani cities of Rawalpindi and Peshawar. Here, the river's current is dammed, creating the Tarbela Reservoir. After leaving the reservoir, the Indus enters the plains of Punjab and Sindh Provinces. The river's pace slows, and its path becomes wider and occasionally divides into smaller channels that lead to the Arabian Sea. Finally, the river passes by a city, Hyderabad, which was well known for producing perfumes in pre-Pakistan times. The watercourse ends in a large delta southeast of the world's sixteenth-largest city, Karachi. Many conservationists consider the ecological region of the delta one of the world's most important.

Tributaries of the Indus include the Jhelum, Chenab, Ravi, Beas, and Sutlej Rivers. The life-giving qualities of these tributary rivers are apparent as inhabitants carve terraces into mountain slopes in order to plant crops. As the Indus flows toward the Arabian Sea, the riverbanks widen and the river flows more slowly, creating a wide delta that contains rich soil. The Indo-Gangetic Plain, which is 186 miles wide north to south and 1,864 miles long east to west, contains Bangladesh and Bengal in the east, the mid-Gangetic Plain and Delhi-Agra territory in north-central India, and the Indus River valley in the northwest. This is the fertile land that has tempted numerous invaders to enter the subcontinent. This is also the region that, after luring wandering groups of combatants, tamed many of these nomads into following an agricultural way of life. In many respects, the villages that grew out of this "taming" process represent the distinctive traits of Indian culture.

The name Indus is a derivative of the Sanskrit word *Sindhu,* which means "a large body of water, a sea or an ocean."[9] Ancient poetry of India refers to the Indus as "King River." The Indus in Greek and Latin is "Sinthos" or "Sindus," respectively. Over time, the name of the river came to represent the people who lived beyond the river—the Hindus—and India is named after the river. Arrian, the Roman writer who chronicled Alexander the Great's exploits in India, viewed the river as the boundary of India, calling all land east of the Indus "India" and all peoples east of it "Indians." Indeed, it is from this river "whence the land gets its name."[10]

Today, the Indus River belongs not to India but to Pakistan, a country with a population of approximately 150 million people. More than half of these people live along the Indus River valley, relying on the water the river supplies for irrigation, drinking, and other purposes. Major Pakistani cities located in the Indus River valley include Faisalabad, Lahore, Rawalpindi (or Islamabad), and Peshawar. Without the river, the people living in this region could not sustain themselves.

THE ANCIENT INDUS PLAIN

Geologists, backed by considerable scientific evidence, now believe that another ancient river, the Saraswati (sometimes called the Ghaggar-Hakra), once flowed next to the eastern border of what is now the Indus Plain. Conversely, the ancient Indus River bordered the western edge of the same plain. The ancient Indus, much like its still-flowing descendant, entered the Arabian Sea in a wide delta near the modern city of Karachi. The Saraswati might have deposited its waters into the Arabian Sea in the salt flats of the Greater Rann or it may have joined with the Indus on the wide and sprawling Indus Delta. The Saraswati was viewed as a vital river and was described by the Rigvedic Aryans in the following manner:

> Foremost mother, foremost of rivers, foremost of goddesses, [Saraswati]. In thee, [Saraswati], divine, all generations have their stars.
>   Yea, this divine [Saraswati] terrible with her golden path, foeslayer, claims our eulogy. Whose limitless, unbroken flood, swift-moving with a rapid flush, comes onward with tempestuous roar.[11]

The swift-moving waters of the "foremost of rivers" proved to be less than limitless and capable of being broken, however. It is not known what caused the river's demise—possibly tectonic shifts. Whatever the cause, the Saraswati eventually stopped flowing. Ancient Indians recorded this occurrence in Vedic and Brahmanical writings.

By the late nineteenth century, geologists such as R.D. Oldham had started to diagram the ancient rivers by mapping the dry riverbeds of the Punjab Province. This mapping demonstrated "how the drying up of the Saraswati had led to numerous stream channels."[12] The Sutlej, which had been one of the major tributaries of the Saraswati, was eventually acquired by the Indus, and it still feeds into the Indus today.

Ancient Indians attempted to explain the shifting nature of the Saraswati. In some accounts, the river simply disappeared beneath the sands of the Punjab. A later explanation described the river as a goddess who continually altered her course and created new channels in order to provide water for all of the upright and virtuous people living in the region. Likewise, there are also stories that detail the changing courses of the Sutlej.

ANCIENT PEOPLES

Many Stone Age archaeological sites have been discovered throughout the subcontinent of India. All have been dated to less than 500,000 years ago, making it likely that the ancient relatives of *Homo sapiens* did not arrive any earlier. Most of the Stone Age sites have been identified near water sources, such as along riverbeds and lakes, and on the perimeter of jungle or desert lands. In some cases, evidence suggests that some of these areas were inhabited only part-time, for instance, during the rainy season, when plant life was plentiful and wildlife would have gathered at watering holes. These wandering hunter-gatherers probably lived in small groups.

Excavations have revealed a change in the kind of tools used in this region about 20,000 years ago. Instead of using the multipurpose stone axes that characterize the Stone Age, inhabitants began crafting smaller, lightweight stone tools

The Sutlej River, shown here near Tholing, Tibet, is one of the Indus' major tributaries. The Sutlej's source lies in southwestern Tibet, and it serves as the border between India and Pakistan for a 65-mile stretch before joining up with the Chenab River in Pakistan, where the two rivers flow into the Indus.

fitted with handles and designed for specific tasks. These tools could be sharpened and included arrowheads, scrapers, and axes. Although the use of Stone-Age tools continued for some time, the Indian subcontinent occupants began to advance technologically.

Evidence also suggests that the nomadic lifestyles of the past began to give way to a more settled way of life. This can be seen in some of the dwelling sites that have been discovered. Individuals began to live in caves or cave-like structures. Economically, it seems that hunting-gathering led to less reliance on hunting or fishing (although these practices continued) alone as the settled people started limited trading (probably bartering), some degree of farming, and relatively simple modes of domesticating animals.

Cave art from about 10,000 years ago still survives in the region, indicating the desire for artistic expression. Such art might also hold some religious significance, but its true meaning is uncertain. The art discovered includes depictions of people and animals, as well as activities such as hunting and fighting. Others are believed to illustrate the universe as the local population viewed it. Because the only records of people at this time are a few artifacts and pictures drawn on cave walls, it is difficult to gain a clear understanding of what their lives were like. For peoples living after 7000 B.C., however, proof of their existence in settled societies increases.

One such settlement, Mehrgarh (located on the Bolan River in Baluchistan), which lies on the edge of the Indus Plain, appears to have been inhabited for more than 4,000 years. Buildings were erected with mud bricks. Pottery, at first made by hand around 5000 B.C. and with the help of the potter's wheel around 3500 B.C., was common and included many kinds of containers that were used for a variety of functions. This distinctive red pottery was decorated with black dyes. Wheat and barley were cultivated for consumption and were harvested with stem-cutting tools first made of stone and later of copper. Domesticated animals such as sheep and goats were common, as were cattle—the latter by around 4000 B.C.

What is distinctive about these archaeological finds is not the bricks, pottery, evidence of plant domestication, or animal husbandry. Similar sites have been found in other places even on the Indian subcontinent. Rather, it is the time period in which these settlements on the Indus Plain came into being. The Mehrgarh settlement predates the first known Indus Valley community by several hundred years. These archaeological finds also demonstrate that ancient peoples could sustain themselves and fashion a society in the region if they settled near a reliable water source. The Indus River valley, with the river's consistent and slow-moving flow and the valley's level, fertile plain, was ideal for the development of a civilization—one would rise up in the region in the middle of the third millennium B.C.

2

The Indus Valley Civilization

The Indus Valley civilization is one of four early civilizations that came into being at about the same time. The Mesopotamian and Egyptian civilizations can be traced to about 3000 B.C., and Shang China is usually dated at 1776 B.C. The beginning of the Indus civilization falls between its Middle East and Far East counterparts, with most scholars placing it no later than between 2600 and 2400 B.C., although some date its beginnings to about 3000 B.C. In addition to originating at roughly the same time, the Indus civilization shares other similarities with its counterparts. First, each of the ancient civilizations was located near a fertile river valley: Egypt on the Nile, Mesopotamia on the Tigris and Euphrates, and Shang China on the Yellow. Second, the river valleys of the Mesopotamian and Egyptian civilizations, like the Indus civilization, were set between mountains, desert, and sea. In each of these early societies, the development of techniques for controlling water, such as dealing with floods and digging irrigation canals, was essential to sustaining a population. Third, each of the four early civilizations centered on the ability of its population to employ intensive agriculture to feed its residents. Finally, although the Egyptian, Mesopotamian, Indus, and Shang China civilizations managed to produce adequate food supplies, each relied on trade to furnish many other necessities not easily found or produced in their respective regions. These commodities included products such as wood and metals, vital components in crafting tools, jewelry, or other cultural artifacts.

Despite being one of the earliest civilizations, the Indus Valley civilization left no discernible written record of its grandeur—thus far, scholars have been unable to decipher the Indus script. Archaeologists therefore hold the key to understanding this ancient culture. This is sometimes accomplished by comparing the Indus Valley civilization to civilizations in South Asia and even Mesoamerica.

THE FIRST PEOPLES

Although it originated at roughly the same time as the other ancient cultures already mentioned, and shared the characteristic of being located within a river valley, the Indus civilization did not have a lasting influence on subsequent peoples. Each of the other three societies, although replaced by later peoples, retained much of their culture and succeeded in altering new-comers and conquering peoples. The Indus civilization, however, rose, flourished, and vanished with few remaining traces. Later civilizations did surface and thrive on the Indian subcontinent, but they appeared on the Ganges River, not the Indus.

Scholars believe that human communities have existed throughout the Indian subcontinent for 500,000 years. This idea is bolstered by the discovery of Stone-Age sites in virtually every part of the subcontinent. These sites have been estimated at between 150,000 and 400,000 years old.[13] According to this interpretation, "middle Stone Age" societies emerged 10,000 to 40,000 years ago. As discussed in chapter 1, communities began to appear in the valleys and river plains around 7000 B.C. The importance of establishing communities near water cannot be overstated. Modern excavations in the region have discovered more than 1,000 sites, nearly all of which are situated on rivers and streams. Thus, the founding of urban centers next to the Indus is not surprising.

HARAPPAN CIVILIZATION

The Indus Valley civilization is called by several other names, including the Indus civilization and the Harappan civilization. The name Harappan comes from the name of the first discov-ered city of this ancient society. The Harappan culture came into existence no later than about 2600 B.C., possibly 400 to 600 years earlier. It is believed to have been the largest civiliza-tion in the world until about 1500 B.C. The culture was spread out over a large geographic region and appears to have been very peaceful. Trade was prominent, more so than either the practice of agriculture or making war.

The urbanized Harappan culture was extensive throughout the Indus Valley region. Remnants of Harappan civilization are "scattered over an area no less than about half a million square miles," and they include more than 70 population centers.[14] The civilization's size was more than twice those of the ancient Mesopotamian and Egyptian civilizations. Despite its vast size, the Harappan civilization was unique because of its uniformity. All through the region, in large walled cities or small villages, excavations have revealed standardized bricks used in building. Archaeologists have also discovered standardized weights in virtually every part of the Harappan civilization area.

The rise of the Harappan civilization marked the development of urban centers and their accompanying traits. Specifically, with urbanism came division of labor, specialization, and technological innovations that made life somewhat easier and more enjoyable for inhabitants of the growing cities. One innovation was the uniform baked bricks mentioned previously, which were used for a variety of purposes. It seems as if almost nothing was constructed without them. Later, these bricks were no longer sun dried but instead were baked in kilns. This served to make them stronger and lengthen their usability. Even more impressive was the fact that these bricks were uniformly made. There were different sizes, but the proportions were almost always 1:2:4 units. In Harappa, the smaller mud bricks—including those that predate kiln-dried bricks—were 7 by 14 by 28 centimeters. The larger bricks, found in the city walls, were 10 by 20 by 40 centimeters. After the introduction of the kiln-baked bricks, around 2600 B.C., the smaller brick size became more common and eventually replaced the larger bricks.

These bricks were among the first clues of an ancient civilization noticed by Westerners in the nineteenth century. With the introduction of the railroad to the Indus region, some British engineers noticed that the local workers were supplying crushed brick for the roadbed. Although crushed brick was as effective as crushed rock, it did raise some questions. On investigation, the British discovered that there were ruins nearby that the locals routinely raided for their abundance of bricks. Excavation did not begin in earnest until the twentieth century, but the unearthing of bricks in large numbers led archaeologists to some of the early finds. It is believed that these same bricks were used to construct large structures (including two-story buildings) and streets, and even to line drainage systems, indicating the use of running water and sewage systems. In fact, these drainage systems included covered drains and allowed houses to be connected to the centralized draining system.

Excavations of the Harappan civilization also indicate the presence of a strong centralized governing authority. This is evidenced in the similarity of buildings, walls, and streets and the layout of city blocks. The cities of Mohenjo-daro and Harappa, both located on the Indus River, were well planned. Each of these cities had paved roads, a granary, and a central fortress. Mohenjo-daro also had a great bath. Indian historian N.N. Bhattacharyya asserted that "the twin cities Harappa and Mohenjo-daro must have served as the twin capitals of the empire."[15] (For additional information on this ancient city, enter "Mohenjo-daro" into any search engine and browse the many sites listed.)

Who comprised this ruling authority? Little definitive proof exists, but some theories put a class of priests or perhaps a monarch who ruled by divine right in power. Historians have proposed many different thoughts concerning this culture, but not even the form of government can be verified. Several revealing facts are known, however. First, the Harappan population was "heterogeneous" and composed of "different

The Indus Valley civilization, which flourished between 2500 and 1900 B.C., was centered between the twin cities of Mohenjo-daro and Harappa. Mohenjo-daro (the ruins of which are shown here) was an agricultural city of approximately 35,000 to 40,000 residents that had paved roads, a granary, and a central fortress.

racial types," principally "Mediterranean, Proto-Australoid, and Alphinoid."[16]

Second, Harappan society was segregated into different classes. N.N. Bhattacharyya described how the architectural remains bring to light the differences in wealth: "The rows of mud brick tenements contrast visibly with the spacious two-storeyed [sic] houses comprising courtyards, bathrooms, private wells, etc., which accommodated what may be termed as the Harappan bourgeoisie."[17] Generally, the houses that have been uncovered are of a standard size, with large doors and no windows.

Third, evidence suggests the presence and development of professionalism. This is substantiated by the discovery of objects used in daily life. These objects would have been used for a wide range of activities and occupations, including agricultural production, artisan craftsmanship, commercial trading, administration and ruling, and religious ceremonialism. These discoveries have led many to conclude that division of labor and the growth of professionalism existed in Harappan society.

Fourth, as mentioned previously, archaeological finds confirm "the uniformity of weights and measures all over the area, the similarity of seals, the evidence of extensive trade, the common elements in architecture and town-planning and also in art and religion."[18] Examined together, this evidence makes it difficult to deny the existence of at least some form of centralized authority, although some if its identifying character traits might not be known. Collectively, all of these individual facts "suggest political, economic and cultural unity of the Harappan civilization and the existence of a functioning state system."[19]

These facts concerning the Harappan culture have led to differing interpretations of their significance and meaning. The fact the Harappan civilization had a heterogeneous population with divisions within it gives weight to the argument that the Aryans (who will be discussed later in the chapter) were not invaders but rather were a group from within the existing culture who came to dominate after other, irrepressible circumstances weakened the civilization. The development of professionalism and the existence of uniform products might simply be evidence of a well-established trade system—not a centralized government or ruling authority. Others argue that, because the Indus civilization displayed such uniformity, a centralized group of people, such as a group of priests, must have ruled collectively. Despite the unearthing of many buildings at many different sites, not a single temple has been uncovered, which stands in marked contrast to the ziggurats (pyramid temples) found in Mesopotamia. Thus, without new discoveries to shed light on the people who lived in this region at that time, Harappan history will continue to be strongly debated by scholars.

No textiles have been discovered, but archaeologists have found many spindles, indicating that the spinning of cotton and wool took place. A great many of these spindles and spindle-wheels exist, suggesting that the practice was common. Dyeing, evidenced by dyers' vats, was also performed.

Thus far, none of the discovery sites have revealed paintings. The only examples we have of drawing and painting by the Indus people comes in the form of animals, birds, and geometric designs found on pottery. Although some of the discovered pottery is well made, much of it is somewhat crude. Likewise, many of the pictures found on this pottery are of lower quality than those found in Mesopotamia. Archaeologists have also found a small number of stone statues and at least one made of bronze. Some of these are finely crafted pieces.

In large part, the success of the Harappan cities is attributable to the region's capacity to produce large amounts of food. The river system provided irrigation and allowed for easy transportation of crops and other items necessary for a thriving trade relationship. Not only did the Harappan cities trade within the subcontinent, but they also established trade relationships with places as far away as West Asia in the east and Mesopotamia in the west.

THE DECLINE OF THE HARAPPANS

The Indus River cities and surrounding area formed a prosperous, thriving society from 2500 to roughly 1900 B.C. The situation changed around 1900 B.C., and scholars debate the cause—or causes—for the decline. Some have concluded that mudslides altered the course of the Lower Indus and restricted irrigation to the extent that the urban populations could no longer sustain themselves. Others think that the mudslides helped form swamps, which allowed the resulting increased

(continued on page 24)

INDIAN WRITING

One of the most discussed and debated topics related to the Harappan civilization is that of writing. The Indus people wrote with seals, which is accomplished by imprinting wet clay with different shapes. This form of writing died out in the region with the demise of the Indus civilization. Thousands of these seals have survived, but archaeologists and historians face something of a mystery: The seals cannot be deciphered!

Although scholars have had these seals, the so-called Indus script, since the early twentieth century, little progress has been made in decoding their meaning, largely because of the nature of the seals themselves and the problem of language. All of the known texts are extremely brief: The average text length of the seals is just five symbols. In fact, the longest known text length is only 26 symbols! Other problems that relate to language also complicate translation. First, modern scholars do not know the original language—they even disagree as to what the language is. Some claim it is Aryan, others a form of Dravidian, or possibly a language belonging to the Munda family of languages from Southeast Asia. To others, the language is apparently unrelated to any known language (called an "isolate"). Thus, scholars have little to work with in deciphering the seals. When one or a group of scholars does declare a breakthrough, many competing scholars find fault with the new interpretations.

Second, no segments of this writing found to this point include parallel passages in a known language. Scholars have translated other ancient writings, such as Egyptian hieroglyphics, by using a known-language translation of the unknown ancient writing. In other words, there is no "Rosetta Stone" that has been discovered and may be used for translating the Indus script.

Other obstacles presented in translation attempts include the number of symbols used in the script. The Indus script may use as many as 400 different symbols. Alphabetic systems usually have fewer than 40 symbols, so it is unlikely that the Indus script is an alphabetic system. Similar analysis rules out Indus being classified as a syllabic system, which would normally have 40 to 100 different symbols. An example of a syllabic system is Linear B, an ancient Mycenaean form of Greek, the oldest known dialect of Greek. Instead of being syllabic, it is likely that the Indus script is either a logophonetic (signs are used to convey meaning and phonetic value) or logographic (signs represent actual words) system, each of which utilizes

In order to communicate, the Harappan civilization used stone tablets that contained pictograph writing like these found at Mohenjo-daro. Symbols like these could be used to represent several different words, but scholars have been unable to decipher their meaning.

hundreds or even thousands of symbols in writing. The Indus script has about 200 basic symbols, and twice that many that are combined from other signs, probably identifying it as a logophonetic system.

There are some limitations and interesting challenges in a logophonetic system. What are the rules for what represents what? Often, these pictorial depictions are misnamed "pictograms"; they are more appropriately termed "logograms" because they represent words in the language:

> However, it's next to impossible to write out a word with abstract meaning pictorially. What all early writers figured out was to use a logogram not for the object or idea it was originally supposed to stand for, but for all words sounding similar to the original word for that object or idea. For example, in English to write "leave" we can use a picture of a "leaf." This is called rebus writing, and is a tremendously common pattern in all early writing systems. We could also then use the same "leaf" symbol to stand for the sound in "relief," adding another symbol in front of the "leaf" symbol in order to indicate the "re" sound. So the logogram gained a phonetic value as well.[*]

Thus, how the language was used also hinders attempts to translate the Indus script. In English, we all "know" what the unwritten rules are in order to read, write, and communicate with one another. In the case of an ancient, dead, and unknown language, what are those unwritten rules that give the necessary cues for comprehension?

The Indus script might hold the key to discovering what happened to the Indus Valley civilization. Until the obstacles of deciphering it are overcome, the script itself will remain as mysterious as the disappearance of its people.

[*] AncientScripts.com. Indus Script: *http://www.ancientscripts.com/indus.html.*

(continued from page 21)

mosquito population to spread disease, most likely malaria, which in turn negatively affected the population. Still others believe that the irrigated land on which the Indus Valley civilization had built its hopes became nonproductive because of increased levels of alkalinity—much as had happened to the land in Lower Mesopotamia.

What else could explain the disappearance of the Indus Valley civilization? Perhaps it is as simple as the harshness of the Indian climate. A British historian, Thomas Babington Macaulay, who served in Calcutta on the Supreme Council of the government of India for a time during the nineteenth century, described the effects of the Indian environment:

> One execrable effect this climate produces—it destroys all the works of man with scarcely one exception. Steel rusts; pins become quite useless; razors lose their edge; thread decays; clothes fall to pieces; books moulder [sic] away and drop out of their bindings; plaster cracks; timber rots; matting is in shreds. The sun, the steam of this vast alluvial tract, the infinite armies of white ants, make such havoc with buildings that every house requires a complete repair every three years.[20]

Whether the natural disasters were localized or widespread or even began this decline, another factor had a profound impact. In approximately 1500 B.C., the Aryan invasions, possibly coupled with natural disasters, succeeded in transforming the society of the peoples living in the Indus River valley.

THE ARYANS

Either causing the decline or following the decline of the Indus Valley civilization, a group known as the Aryans began to dominate northern India. The Aryans might have come from the north and west (from present-day Iran and Afghanistan) and entered the Indian subcontinent through the Khyber Pass. The invading forces were one of the earliest peoples of ancient Asia to successfully breed horses. Like those of other horse-breeding peoples of the time, the Aryans' hostile actions often frightened and intimidated neighboring cultures into submission. This theory has long been taught and accepted; it rests on the belief that the Aryans were nomadic and managed to defeat the Harappan civilization through superior weaponry (made of iron), chariots, and tactics.

Others believe that the Aryans were simply one of the groups already living within Harappan civilization. This is explained by tracing similar movements of people such as the Achaeans (into Greece) and the Kassites (into Sumer) at about the same time (1900 to 1750 B.C.). This theory contends that the Aryans were already a part of the Harappan civilization and simply grew into a powerful force and came to dominate the other groups within the culture. Scholars who believe this explanation point to excavations, which thus far have failed to produce evidence, such as iron weapons, that the invasion hypothesis would require. These excavations also indicate that natural occurrences such as floods might explain the decline of the Indus River civilization.

The lines of disagreement, then, are obvious: Either the Harappans and Aryans lived peacefully together within one society, at least for a time, or the Aryans entered the region as conquerors, established themselves as the ruling class, and set up the caste system to strengthen their power. Archaeologists and historians are increasingly accepting that the Harappan culture had already died out or at least had begun to deteriorate, perhaps as recent as 1750 B.C. The formerly nomadic Aryans became a settled people, raising cattle and nurturing crops. They imitated the Harappans in many ways. Thus, it is likely that the Aryans *replaced* the Harappan civilization and did not drive them out as previously believed.

3

The Vedic Age

The Aryans referred to themselves as the "noble" or "superior" ones. The names of their tribes or their leaders are not known. They spoke an early form of Sanskrit, an Indo-European language distantly related to Latin, Greek, and Celtic (and their modern descendants such as English), and closely related to ancient Persian:

> The Sanskrit *nava*, "ship," is related to the English word *naval; deva*, "god," to divine; *raja*, "ruler," to *regal*; and so on. The word *Aryan* itself comes from *Arya*, "noble" or "pure" in Sanskrit, and has the same root as Iran and Eire.[21]

These noble people evidently turned their backs on the superior advancements of the Indus people. This may be accounted for in part by the nomadic nature of the Aryans, who assessed wealth in cattle. The importance of cows is still seen in Hinduism today.

THE HOLY WRITINGS OF HINDUISM

Unlike that of the Harappan civilization and the transition between the Harappan and Aryan cultures, scholars have fairly extensive knowledge of the Aryans because they left written records, even though these sources were compiled much later. A great deal of what is known of the Aryans comes from the Rig-Veda, one of the four Vedas—a collection of books that contain hymns or verses that form the liturgy of ancient Hinduism. The ideas contained within the Vedas were so influential that historians refer to the era they were written in as the Vedic Age. (For additional information on the oldest Hindu religious scripture, enter "Rig-Veda" into any search engine and browse the many sites listed.)

The Vedas were written in Sanskrit and compiled between approximately 1500 and 500 B.C. The Rig-Veda, the most important of the Vedas, is a compilation of more than 1,000 hymns that contain philosophical discourses, Hindu mythology, and ritual texts. According to the Vedas, the Aryans invaded northern India and conquered the Indus Valley civilization. Scholars believe that the Vedas are written copies of oral traditions passed down to many generations over a long period of time, meaning that much of early Indian history is somewhat unclear—because dates of specific people and events are only an approximation. Because the Vedas were recorded many years after actual events, it is likely that there is some embellishment that makes the Aryans appear as conquering heroes. The Rig-Veda, which is the oldest of the Vedas and was written by the Aryans, is believed to have been completed around 1200 to 900 B.C. Some time later, probably 800 to 400 B.C., the Vedanta, which is a religious philosophy and the culmination of the four Vedas, was established.

The Vedas were revered as holy texts, but the meaning of life was not specifically addressed in them. As a result, a group who sought to find the meaning of life emerged. In time, these seekers came to believe that something more than the Vedas was required. After profound consideration, these seekers collected the words and sayings of the sages who had imparted their spiritual wisdom and knowledge. This anthology of wise sayings became known as the Upanishads, which literally means "came near to the gurus." The Upanishads not only summarize all of the knowledge within the Vedas, but also act as a commentary. Major themes in the Upanishads include the nature of man and god, the soul and god, man's role in this world, the reason for man's existence, and how true salvation is gained.

The Vedas and the Upanishads are not the same thing: The Vedas are viewed as the true foundation of Hinduism, whereas the Upanishads serve to explain Hinduism. In other words, Hinduism is introduced through the Vedas, but the Upanishads help show the way to enlightenment. Thus, the Upanishads are seen as a necessary addition to the Vedas.

ARYAN SOCIETY

Evidence suggests that the Aryans adopted virtually nothing of the Indus Valley civilization: They did not construct cities or use bricks or utilize drainage systems, as had their predecessors. They did not have a written language for several centuries. Whereas the Harappan culture seemingly had a far-reaching centralized authority, the Aryans were organized into small tribal units. Eventually, these tribes, which had been based on kinship, began to depend on their geographical location. Each of the major territories in modern India—complete with distinct cultural practices and languages—can be traced back to the nations of the Vedic Age. Over time, territorial origin became a central part of one's distinct identity. In fact, this concept of identity based on territorial origin is still used by Indians.

Although the Aryans were conquerors when they first entered India, their culture gradually mixed with the native cultures. The militaristic religion of the Aryans, as found in the Rig Veda, became more focused on rites and meditation rather than on active warmongering. Scholars believe that, by about 200 B.C., this progression was complete, resulting in the Indian culture. The Vedic Age then, is not one of a conquering culture but of cultural melding.

This melding did not ensure peace and harmony. Instead, one impact the Aryans had on the existing peoples of the region was to create a kind of pecking order. These groupings served to provide a place in society for each group and individual. During the Vedic Age, the ruling peoples of the Indian subcontinent began to recognize and highlight various social distinctions within their society. These distinctions, which initially included four different classes based on occupation, eventually developed into the caste system. The Aryans believed that some individuals within society were naturally superior and therefore the masters of the supposedly inferior Indians. The classification of each person into one of four groups, or classes, emphasized the differences between the Aryans and Indians.

The top two classes included the Brahmans, or priests, and the *Kshatriya*, or warrior class. Only Aryans could be a member of these two classes. They represented the power in Aryan society, with the Brahmans initially holding more power than the warrior class. In time, the warrior class developed into the governing class. The bottom two classes were for the so-called inferior Indians. The third class was known as the *Vaishya* and was made up of freemen, farmers, and traders. Most scholars believe that the Vaishya was the largest of the four classes. The fourth class was called the *Shudra* and was made up of serfs or those who were not considered free.

Eventually, this system resulted in classes based on birth. A social system that defines one's identity based on birth is known as a *caste*. A caste controls status and much of daily life. With the exception of the lowest, each caste is given special roles to perform and privileges to enjoy. Duties might include religious functions, prescribed diets, or economic tasks. Privileges usually center on religious requirements or social distinctions. Someone born in a caste system is not allowed to change stations in life—he or she is simply expected to accept his or her place and fulfill an assigned role in society.

> According to the *Rig Veda*, the gods themselves were responsible for the caste system:
> When they divided the [primeval] Man into parts how did they divide him?
> What was his mouth, what were his arms, what were his thighs and his feet called?
> The Brahman was his mouth, of his arms was made the warrior. His thighs became the Vaishya, of his feet the Shudra was born.[22]

This imagery makes the role and place for each part of society clear. Although each section of society has its role, it remains a part of a single body created by a god. The caste system, then, was believed to have been planned and ordained by the gods and became deeply embedded in the Indian culture. Some scholars argue that, because the caste system is strongly rooted in notions of ritual purity and in religion, it may have been started and developed in the Indus civilization. Whatever its source, the caste system lingered and grew more distinct in Indian society. By the time the Greeks invaded India in the early fourth century B.C., there were seven distinct castes as recorded by Arrian: wise men/prophets (ascetics), farmers, herdsmen, artisans and shopkeepers, soldiers, overseers (of government affairs), and governing class. This system of classification lasted until the twentieth century, and some of its impact is still felt today. N.K. Bose described the caste system this way:

> According to the ancient Indian sociologists, the caste system is applicable to all forms of society. Where numerous races meet and mingle, it is possible to [synthesize] them in a greater society by placing them in four basic castes. For the need of society if different groups of persons work according to their capacity and skill in diverse walks of life, and if the society guarantees that the persons concerned and their descendants following their traditional occupations will not die of starvation, the society thus formed by mutual cooperation of each social group naturally becomes more powerful. Apart from this cooperation another assurance was given to the village masses. It was absolute cultural freedom. Every group was allowed to follow their traditional social practices, cults and rituals, laws and customs.[23]

In other words, because the caste system presented a defense against economic calamity and offered the freedom of cultural expression, the dominated population did not rise up against successive groups of invaders. There was no pressing need to do so: Everyone could work his or her assigned duty in the economy and the accepted features of culture (such as art) could still be followed. Thus peace was maintained, prosperity virtually assured, and the preservation of traditional Indian culture guaranteed. The obvious downside to the acceptance of this arrangement is that it rests on a system of inequality. In the long run, Indian society was unable to resist foreign invaders largely because of the lack of unity against such intrusions. Because some in Indian society stood to lose a great deal—and all stood to lose their economic and social identity—many chose not to resist. The lesser the threat to the caste system, the less the resistance to the invading threat.

BUDDHISM

In addition to boasting an established class system, India is also home to many religions, some of which originated there. The Vedic Age witnessed the birth of an Indian religion: Buddhism. Buddhism is a set of beliefs that center on the search for enlightenment. It is believed that its founder, Siddhartha Gautama, was born around 563 B.C. in Lumbini, Nepal. His family was part of the Shakaya clan, of the priestly warrior caste. Siddhartha's father was head of the family, and Siddhartha was to be his heir and enjoy all the benefits—including an expensive education—of being raised in a wealthy, powerful family. After marrying a woman named Yashodhara, who later bore him a son, Siddhartha lived with his parents, enjoying the comforts of life. It seemed to the future Buddha that life was good and he had attained happiness.

Siddhartha had lived a very sheltered life, however, and one day an experience shattered his idealistic world. In one of his few

Like Hinduism, Buddhism was developed in India and spread throughout Asia. Siddhartha Gautama, the Buddha (shown here in the center), championed the "middle way," which calls for one to lead a life that lies somewhere between sacrifice and extravagance.

trips from the protection of his father's palace, Siddhartha came into contact with three individuals who revealed how harsh life can be. He saw the effects of old age and the sufferings of sickness, and he came face to face with death. In one day, Siddhartha saw what many saw every day, but he had never experienced. He became determined to seek and find truth, vowing to sacrifice anything and everything to acquire truth.

At age 29, Siddhartha left his family and fortune, turning his back on his wife and child and rejecting his lawful right to his father's throne. He spent time studying Yogic meditation with two hermits, both of whom were Brahmans. Here, he attained high trance and meditative states but did not discover the truth he was seeking. Because he had lived a life of comfort, he decided to conduct his search for truth by undergoing extreme asceticism, a form of very simple living. He conducted long and rigorous fasts and deprived his body of breath for long periods of time—he pushed his body to the limit. He underwent this training for six years. Although these exercises nearly killed him, he still did not obtain the truth that he sought.

After failing to discover truth through asceticism, Siddhartha ended his fasting and undertook lengthy meditation as a path to understanding. In 528 B.C., on the night of a full moon, under a Bodhi tree, where he meditated facing east, Siddhartha received his revelation. He was 35 years old when he reached enlightenment and became a *Buddha*, or an enlightened one. Immediately, he revealed his truth to the five ascetics. After resting for a few weeks, he went to Deer Garden, where he gave his first sermon, "Turning the Wheel of Dharma."

The newly enlightened one desired to show others the way to enlightenment. He called his message the "middle way," which meant that it was in the middle between sacrificial living and a life of extravagance, between asceticism and indulgence. To spread his teachings, Siddhartha founded a community of monks called *sanga*. He also taught his ways for 45 years as the *Shakyamuni* or the "sage of the Shakaya." The Buddha died at the age of 80.

THE GREEKS

Two hundred years later, another influential group arrived in the Indus region. This time, instead of religious thought serving as the agent of change, invading armies carried new philosophies and cultural features to the area. In his quest to conquer the world, Alexander the Great came to India in 327 B.C. Alexander, whose father, Philip, had united Greece under Macedonian rule, had already conquered the mighty Persians during the early 330s B.C. After crossing the Indus River, the Macedonians defeated the Indian force on the field of battle. Having won the surrender of his adversaries, Alexander faced a possible mutiny. His men were tired of fighting and wanted to return home. The young leader sulked but eventually gave in. In typical fashion, however, Alexander decided to return home in a grand and exciting way: by exploring and mapping the Indus River. Flavius Arrianus (or Arrian) described the Indus as "the greatest river of Asia and Europe, except the Ganges."[24] If Alexander's men would not allow him to conquer any more land, then he would explore the Indus.

One reason Alexander was intrigued with the Indus was because it contained crocodiles. The Greeks had seen only one other river with these creatures, the Nile River in Egypt, and Alexander hoped to discover if the Indus served as the source of the Nile. Instead, the local inhabitants described how the Indus flowed into a great ocean, not into a large river on the African continent. Alexander was not dismayed and carried on with his plan to sail down the Indus with his troops. As the Roman historian Curtius wrote, the young conqueror decided to sail down the Indus to its mouth "that he might look upon the end of the earth, the sea, when he had overrun all Asia."[25] He appointed one of his officers, Nearchus, as admiral of the fleet and commissioned him to conduct exploratory surveys and map the river and region as the flotilla made its way to the sea and eventually westward to the Tigris River.

Nearchus has been described as "one of the most outstanding geographers of ancient times."[26] His description of the Indus is the earliest account of the river and the only one that predates the medieval period. Besides mapping the river, Nearchus' account, which was later recorded by Arrian, offers insight into the religious beliefs, languages, customs, and other cultural traits of the peoples inhabiting the region. Although Alexander and Nearchus quickly determined that the Indus was not the source of the Nile, the decision was made to continue the expedition in the hope of finding an uninterrupted water route between the Mediterranean Sea and India.

While Nearchus and the fleet flowed down the Hydaspes (now called the Jhelum River), a tributary of the Indus, Alexander accompanied his men as they continued on land toward the Indian Ocean. Arrian also recorded that the Indus had two mouths that flowed into the Arabian Sea. These mouths were separated by and contributed to an ever-growing delta, much like the Nile River did. On arriving at the Indian Ocean, Alexander proceeded to traverse the coastline with 12,000 of his men, shadowing the Arabian Sea and the Persian Gulf. In the meantime, Nearchus took a corresponding route at sea with 5,000 men and 150 ships. The admiral eventually sailed into the Persian Gulf and to the mouth of the Euphrates River. His records of the coastline and natural harbors proved to be accurate and reliable for future explorers. After reaching the Euphrates, he successfully completed his voyage by circumnavigating the Arabian Peninsula. This achievement, coupled with his detailed log, notes, and maps, was astonishing for its day and helped the Western world notice India and the Indus River in particular.

THE MAURYANS

Alexander the Great entered Punjab Province in 327 B.C. and managed to gain nominal control over the local population. Because of the restlessness of his troops, within two years he was forced to withdraw from the region. After Alexander's

ELEPHANT HUNTING IN ANCIENT INDIA

When Alexander the Great invaded India and conquered the Indus region, he and his army faced Indian forces that used war elephants. The Greeks were fascinated by these large animals. While fighting and subduing the native population, they observed how the Indians managed to catch and prepare the massive beasts for warfare. Flavius Arrianus, a Roman historian better known by his Greek name, Arrian, recorded the lengths to which the Indians went in order to capture, tame, and train these large animals. First, the Indians chose a level place that lacked shade. Then, a circular ditch 30 feet wide and 24 feet deep was dug, with enough room to allow a large army to camp. The dirt from the ditch was piled on the outside, forming a high wall. The hunters then fashioned hideouts for themselves in the wall, leaving small openings through which they could watch their unsuspecting prey.

Then within the enclosure they leave some three or four of the females, those that are tamest, and leave only one entrance by the ditch, making a bridge over it; and here they heap much earth and grass so that the animals cannot distinguish the bridge, and so suspect any guile. The hunters then keep themselves out of the way, hiding under the shelters dug in the ditch. Now the wild elephants do not approach inhabited places by daylight, but at night they wander all about and feed in herds, following the largest and finest of their number, as cows do the bulls. And when they approach the ditch and hear the trumpeting of the females and perceive them by their scent, they rush to the walled enclosure; and when working round the outside edge of the ditch, they

death in 323 B.C., the Greeks stayed closer to the Mediterranean in building their empire. After 321 B.C., the Indus region was forced to submit to a new power in the area: the Mauryans. The Mauryan Empire was established and led by Chandragupta Maurya, whose base of power was situated on India's other important river, the Ganges. Chandragupta Maurya began to extend his territory by attacking the Greek outposts that Alexander had left. It seems that control of the Indus region was find the bridge, they push across it into the enclosure. Then the hunters, perceiving the entry of the wild elephants, some smartly remove the bridge, others hurrying to the neighboring villages report that the elephants are caught in the enclosure; and the inhabitants on hearing the news mount the most spirited, and at the same time most disciplined elephants, and then drive them towards the enclosure . . . they do not at once join battle, but allow the wild elephants to grow distressed by hunger and to be tamed by thirst.[*]

After allowing the sun to do its work, the Indians again constructed the bridge and allowed the riders to enter the enclosure. Initially, there would be a ferocious battle, as the wild elephants perceived the threat of capture. The lack of food and water allowed the disciplined elephants to overcome the wild ones, however. The riders dismounted and tied the feet of the wild elephants together. Then, the tame elephants "punish the rest by repeated blows"[**] until the exhausted animals fell to the ground.

Finally, the hunters tied nooses around the necks of the subdued elephants and climbed onto the animals as they lay on the ground. To protect the rider, an incision was made with a sharp knife all the way around the neck. The noose was then bound around the wound, causing the elephant to keep its neck and head still to avoid the pain of the wound. This protected the riders and enabled them to control the large animals for training. Thus subdued, the elephants were easily led away by ropes.

[*] Arrian, *Anabasis Alexandri*, 345.
[**] Ibid.

of primary importance to the Mauryan ruler, and by 311 B.C., the Indus was under his rule.

In 305 B.C., the ruler of the Babylonian province and contender for ruler of the eastern half of the Greek Empire, Seleucus Nicator, negotiated a peace with Chandragupta. This treaty was set through an arranged marriage and created an alliance between the two empires. The treaty accomplished this by guaranteeing Chandragupta control of all lands east of Kabul.

Seleucus Nicator received 500 war elephants from his new Indian ally. With his eastern frontier secure, Seleucus Nicator eventually won supremacy over his rivals.

As part of the alliance between Seleucus Nicator and Chandragupta, Seleucus sent an ambassador, Megasthenes, to visit Chandragupta at his court at Pataliputra. What survives of Megasthenes' account sheds light on Mauryan society. According to Megasthenes, Chandragupta owned all the land in his kingdom in a somewhat feudal relationship with his subjects. In exchange for rent and a share of their profits, farmers working the land were defended by Chandragupta and his military. Megasthenes also described a flourishing culture administered by a centralized and efficient bureaucracy, as well as the ever-present caste system.

What became of Chandragupta? According to tradition, he converted to Jainism and became a wandering ascetic. Consistent with Jainist beliefs, Chandragupta gave up all earthly possessions in exchange for a life of poverty. He forfeited his throne to Bindusara, his son, who began ruling sometime during the 290s B.C. When Chandragupta died in 272 B.C., he left a strong empire that spanned large portions of the Indian subcontinent.

The Mauryan Empire is significant because it marked the first time the Indian subcontinent witnessed a substantial degree of political unity. The empire lasted until 187 B.C., maintaining its independence through political unity. The state owned and administered important parts of the economy, such as farms, mines, munitions, and spinning industries. According to long-standing custom, the army was divided into four groups: infantry, mounted cavalry, chariots, and elephant riders. Mauryan armies were large: Chandragupta's army supposedly numbered 600,000 men. Many different belief systems (including the Ajivikas, Brahmans, Buddhists, Jains, and others) apparently coexisted peacefully under

Mauryan rule. The Mauryan policy toward religion was generally one of tolerance. Society was segregated into seven distinct groups: philosophers, peasants, herdsmen, traders, soldiers, government officials, and councilors. Because of the relative stability of the Mauryan Empire, its rule is often referred to as one of the golden ages in Indian history: a period in which the country was both independent and united.

Bindusara ruled until his death in 268 or 267 B.C. His son, Ashoka, the most impressive of the Mauryan rulers, succeeded him. Ashoka went about expanding his empire, attacking the kingdom of Kalinga, which lay on the eastern coast of India. According to ancient accounts, Ashoka defeated Kalinga, killing 100,000 men and forcing at least another 150,000 to relocate within the Mauryan Empire. The carnage was so horrific that Ashoka became a Buddhist, rejecting any future use of violence to achieve his aims. Instead, he relied solely on his moral authority for future victories.

Ashoka's decision to convert to Buddhism had far-reaching consequences. Although all religions were tolerated, it is apparent that Ashoka preferred Buddhism, which, with the king's support, became a dominant religious force. He sent Buddhist missionaries to what are present-day Libya, Egypt, Macedonia, Syria, and Southeast Asia. He commissioned his son, Mahinda, to evangelize Sri Lanka. Ashoka successfully managed to politically integrate most of the subcontinent and introduce Buddhism throughout his realm.

To promote a moral society, the reformed ruler set about instituting a uniform and widespread system of fair government. He made the necessary arrangements for public health care, for both his subjects and the animals within his realm. He also initiated agricultural and horticultural innovations, provided protected lands for wildlife, and supported the excavation of caves that later served as shelter for ascetics and traveling monks. To further promote morality, Ashoka issued

Ashoka was the most successful Mauryan emperor; uniting India for the first time in the third century B.C. However, after defeating the eastern Indian kingdom of Kalinga, he converted to Buddhism and renounced war. Ashoka did not force his religion on his subjects; instead he used pillar edicts (shown here), which were written in Brahmi, the first Indian script, to spread his beliefs.

decrees that were to be standardized throughout the empire. These edicts were carved on stones and pillars and placed throughout the Mauryan territory. The pillars were made of sandstone and included Buddhist symbols such as the wheel and the lion. On the top of each pillar were four lions, which still serve as the national symbol of India. Representatives of Ashoka, so-called inspectors of morality, traveled around the countryside, ensuring that his statutes were followed. His administrative and judicial reforms helped guarantee the consistency he sought as he tried to improve the morality of his people.

When Ashoka died in 233 B.C., his kingdom was sound enough that it remained strong and continued to operate as it had for approximately 50 more years. The empire eventually collapsed from the strains of in-fighting and foreign coercion. At the time of his death, Ashoka controlled more of the Indian subcontinent than any preceding sovereign. So much of India would not be governed by one ruler again for more than 1,700 years, when the Moguls came into power. Between the Mauryan Ashoka and the Muslim Moguls lay centuries of unrest and another dynasty that attempted to rule India: the Guptas.

4

The Gupta Dynasty

After the fall of the Mauryan dynasty in the year 187 B.C., the people living on and near the Indus were governed by local principalities that competed with one another for supremacy. These rival groups included various nomads from Central Asia, as well as remnants of the Greek civilization that lay directly to the west and north of the Indus. The most dominant of these groups proved to be the Kushans, who came from what is now Northwest China. By the second century A.D., they had extended their authority to include at least the northern portions of the Indus, possibly even the entire river region. It is believed that the Kushans controlled the profitable silk trade routes between China and the Mediterranean.

THE KUSHANS

The Kushans' territory was widespread and very diverse, and was reflected in their coinage. One of their leaders, Kanishka, had his coins minted with Chinese, Indian, Parthian, and Roman inscriptions. These same coins included depictions of Buddhist, Greek, Hindu, and Persian gods.

One feature of this period was the influx of new peoples and practices into the Indus region. These newcomers came looking for wealth and opportunities. The introduction of new cultural traits into a well-established culture proved to be a complex process. In part, this was accomplished by technological innovations. One of the most important innovations was the construction of artificial ponds for irrigation purposes. This led to increased use of land for agriculture and thus increased agricultural production. As a result, the population along the Indus River grew. Other innovations led to increased trade ties with other parts of the world, meaning that the population located on the Indus became more connected to other places.

The Kushans ruled by allowing local laws and customs to remain intact—they were interested only in controlling the trade that passed through the region. Consequently, the

Kushan Empire operated less like an empire and more like a group of independent principalities that sustained a trade arrangement. This loose federation managed to maintain some control for the sake of preserving its role in the silk trade but that control proved to be minimal and feeble. Soon, other groups began to challenge the Kushans and to carve out their own spheres of influence within the northern regions of the Indian subcontinent.

THE GUPTAS

This tense and unstable environment lasted until the rise and domination of the Gupta kings in A.D. 320. The Guptas originated in the Ganges River valley and eventually ruled northern India, including the Indus River valley. Under the Guptas, the southern portion of the subcontinent served as vassal states. The Guptas are important because they represent the last time a unification movement in India was led by Indians. In many respects, this is the Golden Age of India's history: Many of the Gupta successes and accomplishments later became the benchmarks by which other Indian rulers and dynasties were compared.

The Gupta dynasty also represents the first period in Indian history from which some firsthand accounts have survived. Most of these accounts are either religious poetry or folklore, but even these are somewhat sparse because of the oral nature of India's dominant religious traditions of the time: Buddhism and Hinduism. For the most part, oral records were not written down until much later—perhaps as late as the sixteenth century —so scholars generally rely on archaeological findings.

One firsthand account that has survived is extremely important. A Chinese visitor, a Buddhist monk named Fa-hsien, who traveled to India in about A.D. 406, recorded some of his experiences and thoughts from his journey. His written recollections provide limited insight into the India of the Guptas, especially that of northern India. According to Fa-hsien,

The Gupta dynasty came to power in northern India in the fourth century A.D. and was the last native group to attempt to unite India. The Guptas oversaw a revival of Hinduism and supported the arts, including that of both Buddhism and Jainism. Shown here is one of the Ajanta cave temples in Maharashtra, India, which are known for their extraordinary Buddhist sculptures and paintings.

India appeared to be a calm, prosperous society with a kingdom efficiently ruled by the Guptas, who were well admired by the citizenry. Fa-hsien also described some of the rules that governed the caste system: When visitors and others "enter towns or markets they strike a piece of wood to announce their presence, so that others may know they are coming and avoid them."[27] The caste system affected virtually every aspect of a person's life:

> An individual in a caste society lives in a hierarchical world. It is not only the people who are divided into higher and lower groups, but also the food they eat, the dress and ornaments they wear, and the customs and manners they practise [sic]. . . .
>
> Each caste has a culture which is to some extent autonomous: there are differences in dress, speech, manners, rituals, and ways of life. . . . The concept of pollution plays a crucial part in maintaining the required distance between different castes. A high caste man may not touch a low caste man, let alone accept cooked food and water from him. Where the two castes involved belong to either extreme of the hierarchy, the lower caste man may be required to keep a minimum distance between himself and the high caste.[28]

Thus, a caste provided one with a sense of identity, but that identity came at a price: One was required to eat, dress, and act in certain ways to maintain standing within the caste.

The Guptas oversaw a revival of Hinduism. Indeed, some of the primary traits of Hinduism were introduced and accepted during this era. The temple became the focal point of a Hindu's social and religious life, primarily because of the introduction of image worship and the devotional *bhakti* tradition. Within Hinduism, there are competing thoughts as to how one gains salvation. Some argue for the pursuit of knowledge, and others believe in the performance of rituals. Bhakti is an approach that relies on religious devotion, or piety, as a means of salvation. Other strains emphasize devotion to a god. Samudragupta, who ruled from A.D. 335 to 380, linked himself with deities by reestablishing Vedic sacrifices associated with his position as king.

THE DECLINE OF THE GUPTAS

Quarrels over rights of succession, coupled with revolts by local figures, led to the decline of the Guptas. By the late fifth century, the Guptas were too weak to repel attacks by the nomadic Huns from Central Asia. As a result, control in northern India was splintered for five centuries. Although there was one short-lived consolidation of power on the Gangetic Plain led by Harsha (A.D. 606–647), the Indus region continued to lack any centralized political power until the Muslims brought it when they began to invade India in the eleventh century.

Thus, Hindu society through much of medieval times was a collection of fragmented states competing with one another for dominance and enlarged land holdings. Fighting between rival kingdoms, principalities, or families was common. Many minor rulers gained power through armed conflict, so war was honored as a virtuous pursuit. Because the acquisition of land was the primary ingredient in achieving higher status, wars were initiated and fought over something as small as a minor insult. These wars were organized into grand displays of a ruler's power and military prowess. This elevation of conflict is seen in literature of the period, in which death in battle was viewed as the utmost honor. The ritual sacrifice of *suttee* (or *suti*), in which the widow of a slain warrior threw herself on the funeral pyre, was also encouraged.

Agriculture in this period was primarily subsistence farming, raising crops solely for food. Some large estates had the capacity to raise crops for commercial purposes, but these were mostly inefficient and unable to capitalize on their size. Despite the fact that Indians exported many items—rice, grains, spices, sugar, dyes, wood, and coconuts—and imported others—perfumes, silk, wax, precious stones and metals, ceramics, medicinal herbs, and metal wares—they failed to receive much of the material wealth from these ventures. This is because Muslims controlled

much of the trade. In fact, cotton, which was a common
agricultural product along the Indus River, saw increased
production after the Muslims brought new harvesting techniques to the region. Some within Hindu society did not care
for this increased contact with outsiders. Thus, the Brahmans
who were opposed to trade simply prohibited any of their class
to participate in foreign trade, foreign travel, or farming.

THE MUSLIM TRADE TIES

Many differences between the Muslim and Hindu cultures
divided people. One Persian scholar, Abu Rayhan al-Biruni,
spent his later life at the court of Mahmud of Ghazni and
reflected on and wrote about the barriers to Hindu-Muslim
interaction. He recognized that language was a significant
hurdle, but the religious differences went much deeper and
hindered communication. Speaking from a Muslim perspective, he wrote:

> They totally differ from us in religion, as we believe in nothing
> in which they believe, and vice versa. On the whole, there is
> very little disputing about theological topics among them; at
> the utmost they fight with words, but they will never stake
> their soul or body or property on religious controversy. . . .
> They call foreigners impure and forbid having any connection
> with them, be it intermarriage or any kind of relationship, or
> by sitting, eating, and drinking with them, because thereby,
> they think, they would be polluted.[29]

The differences between Muslims and Hindus were numerous and ran deep in the cultural identity. Because there was so
little common ground, there was little room for compromise.
Eventually one would come to dominate the other.

India lacked any comprehensive governing authority. With
no centralized power, trade between groups on the Indian

subcontinent slowly crumbled. Instead of investing, many, especially those with the means and the various religious bodies, kept their wealth in reserve. This decline in trade is further reflected in the worsening of India's roads, which fell into disrepair. By A.D. 1200, most of the old trading connections were fading and many of the trade guilds began to die out. Products that left India were mostly going to Muslims. Upward mobility was limited, and prospects of advancing economically were dim. Like so many times in the past, India's resources attracted outsiders—individuals and groups of people intent on taking advantage of the natural resources and people for their own material wealth. Because the land and its potential were known to the Muslim traders, it is no surprise that Muslims soon coveted the region.

MUSLIM INVASIONS

Islam had first been introduced to the Indus region in the middle of the eighth century, and it arrived as a military force beginning in the year A.D. 1000 in the form of pillaging Muslim armies. The Muslim leader Mahmud of Ghazni, whose base of operations was located south of Kabul (in present-day Afghanistan), led at least 17 incursions into India in the first quarter of the eleventh century. According to tradition, Mahmud captured up to six and a half tons of gold on a single raid. It is apparent that he contented himself with plundering the countryside and made no effort to establish a permanent presence in India. Instead, the loot he seized from India allowed him to transform Ghazni into a remarkable city in its day. (For additional information on this Muslim leader who invaded India, enter "Mahmud of Ghazni" into any search engine and browse the many sites listed.)

After Mahmud, India enjoyed a brief respite from the Muslim raids, which lasted until the end of the twelfth century. Then, another Muslim leader, Muhammad of Ghur, began to lead

CHRISTIANITY IN INDIA

In addition to Hinduism, Buddhism, and Islam, Christianity also holds a place in Indian history, possibly dating back to the first century A.D. According to tradition, the apostle Thomas was the first Christian missionary to reach India, perhaps as early as A.D. 52, arriving on India's Malabar Coast (southern India). According to the Christian account, Thomas converted some of the local residents. Among historians, there is a lack of consensus as to whether or not Thomas ever traveled to India, but there is persuasive evidence of a Christian community in southern India by the fourth century. It was then that a community of 400 families from Syria, led by Thomas Cana, settled in southern India. This group established what is now known as the Nestorian Church in Kerala.

India is also home to other Christian religions, including Eastern Orthodox sects. When the British controlled India, authorities feared that the spread of Christianity would lead to a collapse of Indian society, which was predominantly Hindu. Consequently, missionary efforts were discouraged. Today, Christians make up only 2.5 percent of India's population.

attacks into India. Much like leaders of earlier Muslim raids, Muhammad conducted his attacks from Afghanistan. Unlike Mahmud, Muhammad apparently came not to seize booty and return home, but to build an empire. As he conquered, he built mosques—on the remains of Hindu shrines. In A.D. 1192, Muhammad defeated the Delhi rulers and continued to extend his control eastward.

Other than centralized leadership, what can explain the Muslims' success in invading India? First and foremost, the Muslim army was a professional military force that fought to expand Islam. Every newly conquered territory meant an extension of Islam's reach and new converts. These Muslim armies were well equipped, utilizing cavalry armed with bows and arrows and also weapons for hand-to-hand combat. Muslim armies were made up of any

JAINISM

Jainism is traced to a contemporary of Buddha, a wise man named Vardhamana, who was later known as the Great Hero or *Mahavira*. Like the Buddha, Mahavira was born into wealth but renounced it by abandoning his family. He undertook extreme asceticism—a simple lifestyle that embraces self-denial and fasting—that he took to an extreme: He went so far as to reject clothing. He taught that attachment to any object, even clothing, was an attachment to this life and hindered one's search for release from the pain and suffering of this world. Thus, this former man of wealth roamed through India as a homeless, naked beggar.

Also much like the Buddha, Mahavira rejected the dominant religious practice of his day, especially that of animal sacrifice. Mahavira objected by preaching and practicing an extreme form of protest: he advocated nonviolence in any and every circumstance to any creature—but this principle was to be practiced, even if it meant danger or death to the practitioner. This doctrine, known as *ahimsa*, was and is the most recognizable trait of Jainism. It is included in what Mahavira termed the Five Great Vows:

1. No killing under any circumstances
2. No un-truth
3. No greed
4. Total chastity
5. No restrictive attachments to any person or object[*]

These vows are to be followed without exception. Today, Jains habitually "wear gauze masks to avoid inadvertent intake of minute insects and constantly sweep their paths to avoid stepping on some tiny animal or plant."[**] For the same reason, Jains steer clear of moving about in the dark or even bathing. Consequently, Jains are vegetarians even though they are prohibited from farming because it might unintentionally harm a small animal or insect. The ultimate form of sacrifice for a Jain is death by voluntary starvation—the purpose being to prevent harming any other living creature.

Jainist teachings share some traits with Buddhism and Hinduism, especially the concepts of karma and reincarnation. Strains of Jainist ideas, especially that of ahimsa, have influenced both the Hindu and Buddhist beliefs. This is notably evident in the teachings of nonviolence advocated and practiced by Mahatma Gandhi and Martin Luther King, Jr., as they struggled for Indian independence and American civil rights, respectively.

[*] Adler, *World Civilizations*, 190.
[**] Ibid.

number of ethnicities and backgrounds. Even slaves could join and hope to gain access to social mobility through dedicated service.

After their victory over Delhi and establishment of Islamic rule there, the Muslim invaders attempted to extend their influence throughout the rest of the Indian subcontinent. This course of action lasted for about 200 years, but various Hindu leaders in eastern and southern India stopped them short of taking over all of India. Muslim Delhi rulers such as Muhammad bin Tughluq sought to bring the Deccan (south-central India) under control, but the Delhi sultanate eventually lost hold over other portions of its territory, and the Deccan was abandoned except for officials who ruled for Muhammad bin Tughluq at the local level. By 1500, the Deccan was ruled by five independent sultanates who no longer recognized the supremacy of the Delhi sultan. Aside from desires to exercise local rule, the conduct of the ruler in Delhi did not always foster a longing to remain under his regime. At least one contemporary recorded the sultan as harsh and unforgiving:

> During the years of the famine, the Sultan had given orders to dig wells outside the capital, and have grain crops sown in these parts. He provided the cultivators with the seed, as well as with all that was necessary for cultivation in the way of money and supplies, and required them to cultivate these crops for the [royal] grain-store. When the jurist 'Afif al-Din heard of this, he said, "This crop will not produce what is hoped for." Some informer told the Sultan what he had said, so the Sultan jailed him, and said to him, "What reason have you to meddle with the government's business?" Some time later he released him and as 'Afif al-Din went to his house he was met on the way by two friends of his, also jurists, who said to him, "Praise be to

God for your release," to which our jurist replied, "Praise
be to God who has delivered us from the evildoers." Then
they separated, but they had not reached their houses
before this was reported to the Sultan, and he commanded
all three to be fetched and brought before him. "Take out
this fellow," he said, referring to 'Afif al-Din, "and cut off
his head baldrickwise," that is, the head is cut off along with
an arm and part of the chest, "and behead the other two."
They said to him, "He deserves punishment, to be sure,
for what he said, but in our case for what crime are you
killing us?" He replied, "You heard what he said and did not
disavow it, so you as good agreed with it." So they were all
put to death . . .[30]

Thus, the Delhi sultanate ruled the Indus valley with firmness
and little grace.

A nomadic force from the Gobi plains of Mongolia soon
emerged to challenge the Delhi sultanate. The Mongol leader,
Genghis Khan—who eventually conquered much of Asia
and even pushed into Europe—managed to take control
of the Indus Valley in 1221. Later Mongol attempts to
more fully dislodge the sultanate in 1299 and 1306–1307
ultimately failed.

By 1500, India could be described as a collection of mis-
cellaneous cultures and traditions all fused together on
the subcontinent. Hinduism was pervasive in the south,
but Buddhism was scattered throughout the region. Muslims
solidly held the north, but there was little uniformity. The
Delhi sultanate was primarily Turkish, but the Muslim culture
was also influenced by a host of adherents from other Islamic
ethnicities, including Afghans, Iraqis, and Persians. In terms
of political power, the Muslims were practical. Power was
usually divided between the sultan and his military officials.
Because different sultans controlled different areas of India,

different bureaucratic structures were applied, depending on the ruler and often times, local customs. Thus Muslim government in 1500 was extremely diverse. Then a new force within the Muslim world emerged to bring standardization to India: the Moguls.

5

The Mogul Period

The Mogul period is one in which India was again attacked and subdued by foreign forces. It began with the invasion and conquest of northern India by the Chaghatai clan from present-day Uzbekistan. From this clan came a new dynasty, the Timurids, who spoke Turkic. The Timurids traced their lineage back to Genghis Khan and Timur, two of the most celebrated Mongol heroes. The Moguls were the last of the Mongol invaders, but they were quite different from the Mongols of old. The Moguls were converts to Islam, tracing their religious heritage back to the conversion of the Mongols who invaded the Middle East. In many respects, their time in the Middle East had made them more Persian than Mongolian: The Persian word for Mongol is Mogul, hence the name of the empire. That same Persian word is where we get the English word "mogul," which means "tycoon."

The warring ways of the Mongols helped extend Persian culture into India. The Persian culture had at its heart the mysticism of Shi'a Islam. This mysticism stressed a divine light, revealed in this life as a religious guide (the imam). Persian culture was also influenced by Sufi mysticism, which empha-sized a spiritual union between God and humans. The Moguls were not the first to introduce Islam to India, however: Turks, who were also Muslims, had established the Delhi sultanate in the early fourteenth century. Mogul culture also contained aspects of Mongolian heritage, most evident in art that reflects Chinese influences.

BABUR

One of the Timurids, Zahir ud-Din Muhammad (1483–1530), was a great-grandson of Timur, and is better known by his nickname, Babur, which is Arabic for "tiger." Babur, whose mother was descended from Genghis Khan and whose father was descended from Timur, had held hereditary claim to the Uzbekistani principality of Fergana, but he lost the crown

Zahir ud-Din Muhammad, better known as Babur, was descended from the great Mongol leaders Genghis Khan and Timur, and was the first ruler of the Mogul dynasty. After conquering part of what is today Afghanistan, Babur became the first Islamic leader to use muskets and artillery in his campaign to conquer India in the 1520s.

city of Samarkand in 1501. Babur found other territories to conquer and rule, having gained power in Kabul in 1504 after defeating other claimants. He wanted to enlarge his territory, and he desired to conquer India in particular.

One might wonder why Babur sought to conquer India, given his initial impressions of the region and its people when he began his campaign:

> Hindustan is a country of few charms. Its people have no good looks; of social intercourse, paying and receiving visits there is none; of genius and capacity none; of manners none; in handicraft and work there is no form or symmetry, method or quality; there are no good horses, no good dogs, no grapes, musk melons or first-rate fruits, no ice or cold water, no good bread or cooked food in the [bazaars], no hot baths, no colleges, no candles, torches or candlesticks.[31]

This low regard for India was later replaced by the recognition of the wealth of resources that the subcontinent offered. In fact, Babur, who founded the Mogul Empire in northern India, later admitted that he wanted to rule India because it was a large country "full of men, and full of produce" with "masses of gold and silver."[32] The rich diversity of India also appealed to him. He viewed it as "a different world; its mountains, rivers, jungles and deserts, it towns, its cultivated lands, its animals and plants, its peoples and their tongues, its rains, and its winds, are all different."[33]

India in the 1520s was a region in turmoil. At least three different groups were engaged in conflict with one another: recently arrived Afghan tribal chiefs, the Rajputs (land holders believed to be descendants of the warrior class in central and northern India), and Ibrahim Lodi, the sultan of Delhi. All of these groups fought each other, opening the door for Babur to enter India. Because the Afghan chieftains and Babur were both Muslim, their differences were overlooked when the latter began fighting the nonbelieving Hindus. Babur later defeated Lodi completely and managed to temporarily subdue the Rajputs. Before he established the Mogul Empire, however, the Afghan tribal chiefs, the Lodi sultanate, and the Rajputs had become competing interests in the region.

When Babur began to look to conquer the region in the 1520s, India was not united. He invaded Punjab Province three separate times but was forced to withdraw each time. In late 1525, he entered India with a force of 12,000 men. This time, he was successful, in large part because of the fine horsemanship of his army but especially because of the use of muskets and artillery. As the first Islamic conqueror to utilize these weapons, he defeated the Indians and established a more permanent presence. Babur won his empire by relying on firearms, the first such empire to do so. About six months after invading, Babur won the decisive victory of Panipat, in which he faced a much larger force. In this battle, the last sultan of Delhi (Ibrahim Lodi) was killed and Babur claimed Delhi as his own. He later built and dedicated a mosque at Panipat to celebrate his triumph. After his victory, Babur sent his eldest son Humayun to Agra to confiscate the royal palaces and the treasure contained within them. After dividing the spoils in accordance to custom, he instituted his capital in Agra.

It took Babur only four years to complete his conquest. In 1528, the Rajput stronghold of Chanderi fell and Rajput resistance in northern India dissipated. Babur also took steps to establish some permanence for his rule. This was mostly achieved through the construction of new mosques. Two of these, located in the northern Indian cities of Ayodhya and Sambhal, were Hindu religious sites. Such acts demonstrated Babur's supremacy and his desire to gain a foothold in India. In 1530, Babur died, but he did so after having successfully established a dynasty of Muslim Indians—later termed the Mogul dynasty.

HUMAYUN'S REIGN

In the first few years after Babur's death, the prospects that his empire would enjoy lasting success were not very promising.

Humayun, one of Babur's sons, succeeded him in 1530, and though he inherited one of the largest empires in world history, he somehow managed to lose all of it in just 10 years due to rebellions throughout the empire. He then went to Persia as an exiled ruler with no territory, but raised an army, and by 1555 had regained much of his lost territory. This reconquest was nearly complete with the capture of Delhi, but just six months later Humayun died after falling down a flight of stairs. The Delhi nobles managed to keep his death secret for 17 days while they agreed on a successor.

It would be a mistake to say that Humayun's reign, with all of its problems, did not influence Mogul culture. In fact, while he was exiled, Humayun acquired an appreciation and love for Persian culture. This is proven by the cultural tastes (literature, painting, philosophy, and architecture) and governing style (tolerance of diverse views) of his son, Akbar.

AKBAR THE GREAT

Akbar, who would later be called Akbar the Great, finished the reconquest his father had begun. Many scholars view Akbar as the greatest Indian ruler. In 1556, he inherited the throne at age 13. His regent, Bairam Khan, was a Persian noble and Shi'a Muslim who had led Humayun's armies to victory as he made his way toward Delhi. Now, with Bairam Khan's assistance and leadership, Akbar was forced to defend himself against others who desired the throne. After defeating a large Hindu force at Panipat, near Delhi, Akbar followed up with aggressive moves to consolidate the heart of the old empire, winning victories in the Punjab, Rajputana, and Bihar Provinces. Within two years, he controlled most of northern India (Lahore, Delhi, Agra, and Jaunpur) and with it the agricultural supply and center of commerce that could feed and supply an empire. In 1560, Bairam Khan fell from power. By that time, Akbar was sufficiently strong to protect his reign.

In fact, he managed to consolidate much of the remaining power, taking full control of the government. He then continued his conquest of India and Afghanistan. At the time of his death, the Mogul Empire was larger than it had been under Babur, encompassing most of northern India.

Because his empire was so large, Akbar devised a bureaucracy to oversee his dominions. His system proved to be efficient and effective in maintaining law and order while collecting necessary tax revenues. To discourage rebellion, he allowed provinces to retain a degree of autonomy. At the head of each region, he appointed military governors who were responsible for the provincial military and the governance of people within the region. Governors who abused their position of power or exploited the weak and poor faced serious punishments, including death. Given that Akbar appointed the military governors, they served at his pleasure.

Perhaps the most vital part of Akbar's bureaucracy was that of tax collection. It was here that Akbar introduced several improvements over previous systems. Like other rulers before him, he imposed a land tax that was equivalent to one-third of the value of crops produced annually on the land. Akbar altered the way taxes were assessed, however: He levied the tax equally, without regard to caste or position. Taxing nobility was rare, but Akbar did not make an exception: Everyone in the empire paid taxes. In addition, the emperor did away with two taxes that targeted non-Muslims. The first was a tax, termed the *jiziya*, that Muslims had historically assessed to any nonbelieving subjects. The jiziya had caused Indians to resent Muslims. The second was a tax, repealed in 1564, that was levied on Hindus traveling to pilgrimage sites.

Akbar was also inclusive in filling government posts. So many Hindus were appointed to the bureaucracy that, by the time of Akbar's death in 1605, Hindus accounted for nearly a third of

Akbar the Great (right) inherited the Mogul throne in 1556 at the age of 13. Though a Muslim, he was best known for supporting local autonomy, which allowed Hindus to not only practice their religion but also keep their own laws and court system. His son Jahangir (left) continued to expand the Mogul Empire after he came to power in 1605 and encouraged artistic expression during his reign.

the government bureaucracy. As one might expect, these reforms won Akbar many supporters within the Hindu population. Even the Rajput kingdoms, which had always resisted Islamic domination, refrained from open opposition. To strengthen his relations with numerous kingdoms, Akbar married the daughters of the kings. Thus, for political motives, he ended up with more than 5,000 wives. Of these wives, his favorite was a Hindu who bore him a son, Jahangir—his successor.

Perhaps the most impressive administrative innovation under Akbar was that of local autonomy. This was permitted in uniform manner, meaning that Hindu territories also enjoyed a large amount of autonomy. Instead of continuing the typical Muslim practice of treating all non-Muslims as Muslims, holding all to the same laws, Akbar adopted a more flexible system: He allowed the Hindus to preserve their own laws and court system. This approach had critics among the Muslims, but it kept the large Hindu population satisfied. It worked so well that this unrestrictive format served as the model for the British when they developed colonial control of India in the eighteenth and nineteenth centuries.

To a large degree, the stability of Akbar's empire was founded on the idea of religious tolerance. As far as the state was concerned, all religions were to be accepted, which explains the abolishment of the pilgrimage and jiziya taxes. Akbar's practices sought to guarantee justice for all subjects, without regard to religion.

JAHANGIR AND SHAH JEHAN, PATRONS OF THE ARTS

Akbar once claimed that a kingdom that was not experiencing expansion was declining. The latter years of his own reign were largely uneventful, however. Instead of making war and expanding his holdings, Akbar busied himself with the affairs of his already large state. In addition to practicing a mystical form of Islam, he was also a patron of the arts. His

(continued on page 68)

COMPETING RELIGIONS

Hinduism was born in India, but with the rise of the Moguls, India became a permanent home for another of the world's major religions: Islam. Hinduism and Islam have little in common, often resulting in conflict between their adherents. Here are some of the ways in which the teachings and beliefs differ:

HINDUISM	ISLAM
• Polytheistic— belief in many gods	• Monotheistic— belief in one god
• God(s) and creation are indivisible	• God and his creation are separate
• Elaborate rituals in worship	• Simple rituals in worship— emphasis on prayer
• Many icons used in worship	• Use of icons or pictures in worship forbidden
• Music in worship	• Use of music in worship prohibited
• Acceptance of inequality (caste system)	• Belief in equality of believers (for males)
• Emphasis on community	• Emphasis on individual
• Primarily monogamous	• Practice polygamy

These differences are further highlighted when one considers that much of the art produced by these groups is religious in nature (especially the Hindu depiction of various gods), meaning that their unique beliefs become even more distinct in contrast to each other. Differentiations are also stressed because both Hindus and Muslims are forbidden by their beliefs to intermarry or even to eat together. The Muslim views the cow, considered holy by the Hindu, as a suitable meal.

There were some attempts to bridge the differences between Hinduism and Islam during portions of the Mogul period, especially during the reign of Akbar. The Sikh movement is the most notable effort to bring the two religions closer together. Sikhism stressed monotheism and personal devotion, and Sikhs do not believe in the caste system. Although the Sikhs and other movements ultimately failed to bring the two religions closer together, their influence is still visible. Islamic emphasis on monotheism is more pronounced, perhaps in response to the Indian experience in which many gods were competing for converts. Muslims also began to hold saint-like figures from their history in high regard, and marriage was influenced by the caste system. Akbar's tolerance of non-Muslims is probably one of the most obvious examples of Hinduism influencing the Islamic state.

For Hindus, the unity of god(s) was a distinctive characteristic of their beliefs during the Mogul period. Other ways that Islam influenced Hinduism are evidenced in the Sikh and other reform movements that sought to end the caste system. Bhakti, an approach whereby salvation is gained through religious devotion or piety, is also a Hindu concept with foreign roots.

There was some compromise and occasionally each group took an idea or concept from the other, but there has never been wholesale blending of Hinduism and Islam. The fact that the two religions are still clearly identifiable today is a testament to the success of past attempts made by each group to retain its identity. Much has been written about the conflicts between Islam and Christianity, especially in regard to the Crusades, but the conflicts between Islam and Hinduism are at least equally important in defining Islam. In fact, the clashes in India during the Mogul era may be a significant factor in the longevity of the two belief systems: Each had a competing, almost completely opposite worldview from which it could distinguish itself. Consequently, both succeeded in establishing themselves as distinct religions with clear and identifiable traits.

(continued from page 65)

son, Jahangir, succeeded him and ruled from 1605 to 1627. Although Jahangir was not as militarily aggressive as his father, he did bring Bengal (in eastern India) under Mogul control. Following the example of his father, he supported the arts over military conquest: Architecture, literature, painting, and philosophy all flourished during his reign. Because of the growth of artistic expression during Jahangir's rule, some have called this period the age of Mogul splendor.

Shah Jehan, successor and son of Jahangir, ruled from 1628 to 1658. Like his father, he supported the arts, encouraged painting, and promoted Mogul architecture in particular, which remains a hallmark of his reign. Exceptional artistic examples from this period, characterized by its distinctive white marble, may be still seen in the architecture found in Agra and Delhi. One of the most recognizable buildings in the world, the Taj Mahal, was constructed during Shah Jehan's reign.

AURANGZEB

The last great Mogul was Shah Jehan's son Aurangzeb, who reigned from 1658 to 1707. When his father fell ill in 1658, Aurangzeb defeated his brothers in battle and successfully seized power and imprisoned his father in the fortress at Agra. He claimed the title "alamgir," which means "world shaker." In terms of religion, he indeed shook things up. His time in power is one in which the religious tolerance of the past came to an end. In sharp contrast to earlier Mogul practices, lenience for non-Muslims was not permitted. Aurangzeb was an orthodox Muslim who wanted to compel his subjects to follow his narrow and strict brand of Islam. To achieve this end, he singled out the Hindus within his empire. He resurrected the old taxes on Hindus, discharged Hindus from government posts, and set about destroying Hindu temples, monuments, and holy places. He ordered the execution of the guru of the Sikhs after the man refused to accept Islam.

In territorial terms, Aurangzeb extended the Mogul Empire to its largest size. He spent the latter half of his reign attempting to subjugate southern India. Despite his gains, his appetite for more territory resulted in depletion of the Moguls' resources and the uniting of the Marathas (located in the Deccan) into a formidable enemy. Revolts by the Jats, Rajputs, and Sikhs also undermined Mogul authority in northern India. Soon after Aurangzeb's death in 1707, the Mogul Empire fragmented and lost its grandeur, although Moguls continued to rule territory in India until the British unseated the last Mogul, Bahadur Shah II in 1858.

THE MOGULS' LEGACY: ISLAM

The effects of the Moguls on the Indus region cannot be overstated: Islam was introduced to the Indus Plain, where it became a lasting influence. Later disputes on the basis of religious differences grew out of the Hindu/Muslim split that occurred only after the entrenchment of a Muslim state was founded and sustained by the Moguls. Because the British later adopted the Mogul practice of allowing locals to administer government, the spread of Islam along the Indus River had repercussions that would be felt in the middle of the twentieth century.

6

British India

In 1498, Portuguese explorer Vasco de Gama landed in India. Portugal soon established a factory fort at Calicut in order to facilitate trade between Europe and India and India and China. Thus, in terms of trade, India served as the intermediary between Europe and China. Portugal soon expanded its presence in other places appropriately situated on the coast. Although Portugal was first to capitalize on this profitable trade, other Europeans—French, Dutch, and English—soon followed.

In the second decade of the seventeenth century, the English established an outpost in India. Eventually, this led to the formation of the East India Company, which was chartered by Elizabeth I in 1600, and enjoyed a monopoly on all English trade with the subcontinent as per an arrangement with the English government. During the next century, the East India Company increased its presence throughout India. Like the Portuguese, the English managed to use India as a means to establish indirect trade with China and acquire its spices. In the process, the company yielded enormous profits.

BUILDING AN EMPIRE

Initially, it was the French who enjoyed prosperous trade in India. Their presence did not openly conflict with England's interests until discord between the two superpowers turned into a war for empire in the 1750s. William Pitt the elder, who served as the British secretary of state during most of the Seven Years' War, saw the fight as an opportunity to win an empire while depriving France of its own. British success in North America, the Caribbean, Europe, and India took valuable colonies away from France and placed them under British rule. Although the French were allowed to maintain a commercial presence in India, by treaty they could not maintain a significant military presence. The turning point for Britain in India was the Battle of Plassey, fought in 1757.

That victory, won by Robert Clive, who commanded the British forces, ushered in a new era for the British in India, paving the way for the Raj (British rule of India) to dominate. Fighting between the two European powers continued, but by 1761 British rule over India was firmly established. British control of India—first by the East India Company and later by the British government—lasted until the middle of the twentieth century. (For additional information on this British general who established the empire of British India, enter "Robert Clive" into any search engine and browse the many sites listed.)

After having conquered its rival for control of India, Britain spent the next 70 years busying itself in the business of empire keeping. The colonies in America rebelled and were lost in the 1770s and 1780s, and Parliament was forced to deal with an enormous debt and an ever-growing empire that required additional funding. The British did little to expand their grasp on India until the nineteenth century, in part because the East India Company was responsible for erecting an empire on the subcontinent.

MAPPING THE INDUS

In 1831, an Englishman named Alexander Burnes left the island of Kutch—located off the western coast of India—for the city of Lahore, located in India's interior on a tributary of the Indus. Burnes traveled inland via the Indus and Ravi Rivers, a voyage of more than 1,000 miles. He sailed under the pretense of delivering five enormous English dray horses and a grand ceremonial carriage from the British government to the Sikh ruler of the Punjab, Maharaja Ranjit Singh. On the surface, this envoy appeared to be nothing more than a diplomatic mission. But in reality, Burnes performed a much greater objective—he secretly charted the Indus River and determined its strategic and commercial value:

In 1831, Sir Alexander Burnes, who had originally come to India to serve in the army of the East India Company, traveled extensively throughout northwestern India and became the first Westerner to explore the Indus River. He published a narrative on his travels and was recognized by the Royal Geographical Society of London for mapping this region.

Local observers exclaimed that with the knowledge of the Indus river, the British would soon be able to control the entire region. Their predictions came true, and within twelve years the British had conquered Sindh. By 1850 they controlled the Punjab as well, thereby adding the entire Indus river valley to their empire.[34]

Thus, the Indus River was vital to the British effort to gain control of India, which then included modern-day Pakistan and Bangladesh.

Later, in the early years of the twentieth century, a more complete exploration of the Indus region was undertaken, but the lead explorer who conducted the surveys was Swedish, not British. Sven Anders Hedin (1865–1952), a native of Stockholm, became the first Westerner to locate the source of the Indus River. Through his travels, this explorer helped map vast regions of Central Asia. These travels were made possible by funding from the Swedish government, which first sent Hedin to the region as an interpreter on a delegation bound for Tehran (in present-day Iran). Hedin eventually conducted four expeditions in Asia, the third of which took place from 1906 to 1908. On that expedition, Hedin sought to discover the sources of the Indus and Brahmaputra Rivers. Although the Himalayas were fairly well mapped by this time, many believed that the rivers started in the mountains. Hedin's journey led him back and forth through the rough terrain in India and Tibet. In honor of his work, those mountains are now known as the Hedin Trans-Himalayas.

COLONIAL INDIA

In the 1830s, the British knew nothing of the Indus River's source or about the topographical layout of the yet-to-be-named Hedin Trans-Himalayas. Instead, the European power acted on what was known: The Indus was strategically important to winning and keeping control of the region. Compared with colonies or territories elsewhere, the British took a different approach to India. Specifically, the British allowed the East India Company to act on behalf of British interests, allowing Britain to enjoy the fruits of India without having to administer it as a colony.

Despite this technicality, India was subjugated to the same rules as other colonies in the British Empire: English was instituted as the official language of government, and some of the time-honored customs, such as the live burning of widows on funeral pyres, were outlawed. In general, however, the Indians were given a great deal of latitude in keeping their traditional ways. British restrictions on traditional customs mainly dealt with maintaining law and order (ending the religiously sanctioned practice of stealing from and murdering travelers) or promoting individual rights (forbidding infanticide and revoking the ban on remarriage for widows).

As part of the vast economic British Empire, India fared well. Britain brought heavy industry to India, beginning construction on that nation's first railway in 1850. Agricultural production was made more efficient, and the expanding railway system encouraged trade. The British East India Company instituted an arrangement in which it received financial support from many small Indian states in order to maintain its army. States that had preserved their independence gradually lost it because they were required to ally themselves with Great Britain and to contribute funds for the common defense of the country.

Difficulties facing the East India Company soon compromised its hold over the subcontinent and eventually led to the government's official recognition of India as a member of the British colonial system. These difficulties were rooted in the financial returns for the company. Over time, the East India Company began to experience a decline in profits; corruption and rising military costs contributed to the shortfall. In order to increase its revenues, the company raised the taxes used to fund its military. In return, many landowners went into debt to meet the increased tax burden. When landowners failed to repay their loans, lenders seized the property as payment. Together with land speculation, these circumstances produced a consolidation of land holdings: Fewer people owned more of the land. Many of the smaller landowners simply lost their land. To alleviate this problem, the British began widespread clearing of forested lands in an attempt to convert the native poor into an agricultural society by providing more land for farming. This and other underlying factors eventually led to the Sepoy Mutiny and, ultimately, the East India Company losing India to Great Britain.

THE SEPOY MUTINY

India's diverse religious heritage helped play a role in the Sepoy Mutiny and eventually in dislodging the British. A Sepoy was an Indian soldier who was trained, uniformed, armed, and employed by the British East India Company and later by the British army. Although there had been earlier revolts, none were as widespread or as dangerous to British interests as the Sepoy Mutiny. Insensitivities to Hindu and Muslim religious beliefs and practices helped spark the revolt. Hindu troops opposed the introduction of soldiers from lower castes, as well as the hiring of Gurkha (soldiers from Nepal) and Sikh soldiers. The British East India Company had used some of these other groups in the past, but increased integration caused concern and outrage. In addition, the Raj economic policies that resulted in unemployment and forced the families of soldiers into new occupations did not help subdue the restless troops. Finally and most important, newly distributed Enfield rifles required new cartridges that were rumored to be greased with animal fat, specifically cow and pig fat. Soldiers were required to bite off the end of the cartridge in order to load the rifle, so Hindu and Muslim soldiers were faced with breaking their long-held religious beliefs: The Hindus held cows sacred and the Muslims despised pigs as unholy.

In early 1857, the East India Company was forced to disband three Sepoy regiments because they rejected orders to take part in military exercises involving the use of the new cartridges. In Meerut, 85 of the native troops refused to load and fire their weapons, resulting in their confinement. On May 10, 1857, a large number of the remaining Sepoys mutinied and marched on Delhi to proclaim Bahadur Shah II, the last Mogul ruler, India's rightful ruler. By June 1857, 70 percent—90,000—of the Sepoys had openly joined the rebellion. The rebellion was widespread, and Indian forces enjoyed early successes against the British, such as at Lucknow. The British, however, effectively employed their forces of British, Sikh, and Gurkha troops to suppress the rebellion. The entire Punjab, the province in which the Upper Indus flows, remained loyal to Britain, allowing the British to concentrate their efforts on the rebels without worrying about the Indus region. It also confirmed earlier assessments, such as those made after the Burnes expedition, of the strategic importance of the Indus—namely, that Britain could control the region if they held the Indus, and consequently, the Punjab.

COLONIAL GOVERNMENT AND ECONOMY

Although mutiny was pervasive throughout much of India, there were no synchronized efforts to form a nationalist movement to oust the British. British rule survived the 1857 revolt —but nationalist and separatist groups later formed to oppose the British presence in India. Parliament reacted swiftly to the revolt, seizing control of India, proclaiming it a colony, and dissolving the East India Company altogether. Thus, despite

The Sepoys, Indian soldiers who were trained, uniformed, armed, and employed by the British East India Company and later by the British army, rose up in revolt against the British in 1857 in protest to the introduction of soldiers from lower castes and the greasing of gun cartridges with cow and pig fat. The rebels were initially successful in what came to be known as the Sepoy Mutiny, but the British were able to put down the revolt within a year. Though the rebellion failed, Indians did obtain religious freedom and thereafter were admitted to minor positions in the civil service.

the financial problems that forced the collapse of the company, India was economically beneficial to Great Britain.

To oversee affairs in the new colony, a secretary of state for India was appointed by the British cabinet. In November 1858, Queen Victoria bestowed a new title on India's governor-general: viceroy. Through the actions of the parliament and the crown, British policy in India began to take shape. An uneasy partnership between Britain and local Indian authorities emerged: In exchange for loyalty to British rule, local princes, rulers, and landlords were allowed to retain their titles and most of their administrative power. To curb the threat of another uprising, the British army was reorganized, significantly lowering the proportion of Indians to Europeans.

The structure of British colonialism depended on reliable transportation systems. Construction of new railroads prior to the Sepoy Mutiny had provided economic links for parts of India to the British Empire. In fact, towns sprang up along the new rail system in order to meet the requirements for exporting goods from India. To further facilitate expansion of India's role in the larger marketplace, the British improved Bombay's harbor, constructed new roads, and enhanced communication systems throughout the country. Economic policies within the empire did not always serve to help India's poor, however: Britain's products were often machine-made in factories, and Indian craftsmen and artisans fell victim to competition in the new economic climate. These jobless workers were forced into poverty and had to farm in order to survive.

The American Civil War, fought halfway around the world from 1861 to 1865, had an impact on India and its citizenry. With the Northern blockade of Confederate ports, American exports of cotton plummeted. The English textile industry looked for new sources of cotton, and India helped fill that need. Indian farmers shifted from subsistence food crops to the more lucrative commercial crop of cotton. A problem arose, however: With fewer farmers providing food products, famine resulted during a drought in the 1870s.

REBELLION

In terms of social peace and harmony, India appeared somewhat placid, yet tensions were always brewing just below the surface. Many Indians felt that the British mistreated

(continued on page 82)

RUDYARD KIPLING

Today, author Rudyard Kipling is well known for his many stories about India, but he first gained fame as a poet. He also wrote short stories and novels, many of which were set in India. Although only one of Kipling's stories included dramatic scenes on and near the Indus (*Life's Handicap*, which includes a crossing of the river at flood stage), the river represented the northwestern boundary of his beloved India because the partition of Pakistan from India did not occur until after his death. Kipling's writings brought India to life for many readers. One of his more popular works, *The Jungle Book*, was first published in 1894.

Kipling was born into an affluent family on December 30, 1865, in Bombay, India. His father, John Lockwood Kipling, was a professor of architecture at the Jeejeebhoy School of Art. An *ayah* (Indian nurse) helped raise Rudyard and taught him Hindustani as his first language. This same nurse taught the young boy much about Indian customs.

"Ruddy," as his family affectionately called him, was sent to England at age five, where he lived in a rigid, Calvinist foster home where he was subjected to beatings and ill treatment. He later wrote of those painful experiences in the short story "Baa Baa Black Sheep" (in the 1890 novel *The Light That Failed*) and in his autobiography, which was published posthumously in 1937. His foster home experiences traumatized him so much that he suffered from insomnia for the rest of his life. At 12, he was placed in a boarding school, where he remained until 1882, when he returned to India. While in India, he was employed as a newspaper reporter, part-time writer, and assistant editor. His time in India as an adult introduced him to British colonialism, which appears in many of his works.

Kipling endured much heartache in his life: Two of his children died before him. A daughter, Josephine, died unexpectedly at age five in the United States. His 18-year-old son, John, died at the Battle of Loos (1915) during World War I. He later wrote a history of his son's regiment.

Kipling remains something of a mystery: He declined numerous honors, including knighthood, the Order of Merit, and the Poet Laureateship. In 1907, however, he became the first Englishman to win a Nobel Prize in Literature. His presentation speech stated that he was awarded the prize for the "consideration of the power of observation, originality of imagination, virility of ideas and remarkable talent for narration . . ."[*]

Kipling became an avid supporter of the British Empire. His political views on his country's imperialism have sometimes resulted in the suppression of many of his works during the age of political correctness. Because colonialism is now viewed by many as unjust and unacceptable, the literary contributions of an individual who lived in Britain's colonial times—and in a British colony—have often been maligned as at best insensitive or at worst bigoted. Kipling was a product of the British Empire, however, born in India within a decade of the Sepoy Mutiny. In his perspective of British colonialism, the poorer, less-developed nations benefited from Britain's advanced technology, a first-rate system of administrative bureaucracy, and the collective defense from affiliate states. His political views exalting Britain even transcended his personal life: Although he married an American and lived in Vermont for a time, Kipling viewed Americans as inferior to the English.

A personal friend of King George V, Kipling persisted in promoting British imperialism until his death in 1936. He believed that it was the responsibility of the developed world to carry "the white man's burden." In a poem of the same name, overtones of racial prejudices explain some of his views on colonialism. His mother country of Britain, however, was destined to lose most of her empire within just a few decades of his death. Kipling is buried in Poet's Corner of Westminster Abbey in London.

[*] Nobelprize.org. Rudyard Kipling—Biography:
http://www.nobel.se/literature/laureates/1907/kipling-bio.html.

(*continued from page 79*)

them. When there were problems, the British often blamed the minority Muslim population. Tensions between the Hindus and Muslims already existed, and the British presence intensified the age-old antagonism. To confront British rule, the Indian National Congress was established in 1885. This group, predominantly made up of Hindus, struggled for the right of self-rule. Britain miscalculated Indian sentiment and, at least initially, largely ignored this group. Soon, however, the congress was enjoying widespread support as it promoted pride in Indian history and products of trade. In 1906, Indian Muslims formed the Muslim League, which defended the right of the British monarchy to rule India. Three years later, under the provisions of the 1909 Indian Councils Act, Muslims won the right to hold separate elections.

As part of their efforts to win World War I, the British fought against the Turks and other Islamic groups in the Middle East. Soon, these conflicts damaged Indian Muslim support of the British crown and talk of establishing a new Muslim state surfaced. In February 1919, the Indian government passed a series of laws known as the Rowlatt Acts. These acts, named after the chair of the committee, who recommended adoption of portions of the temporary wartime legislation, allowed the government to suspend trials by jury and legalized the imprisonment of suspects without trial. The Rowlatt Acts were ratified over the undivided opposition of leading Indian leaders, none of whom held office under British rule. Indians —both Hindu and Muslim—responded to the repressive, now permanent laws by expressing their disapproval of British presence in India. One Indian leader, Mohandas Gandhi, helped organize protests to the legislation.

On April 13, 1919, tensions reached a climax at Amritsar, Punjab District, when British troops confronted a group of about 10,000 people, who were unlawfully protesting the Rowlatt Acts. British troops fired on the unarmed Indian crowd, killing nearly 400 and wounding another 1,200. The incident irreparably damaged Indian-British relations. Nationalist leaders, including Gandhi, refused to cooperate with the British, organized boycotts, refused to recognize the authority of British courts, shunned British schools, and declined to participate in elections. This noncooperation forced the European power to face what had once seemed impossible: Britain could no longer rule India.

The peaceful transfer of power began with Britain allowing the Indians to exercise a large degree of self-government. Then, events in Europe both postponed and hastened the inevitable separation. The viceroy of India declared war on Germany without first consulting the elected Indian parliament, which was controlled by the Indian National Congress. The viceroy's unilateral act led to the resignation of the congress. Although India remained in the war, the end of colonial rule was in sight.

THE TRANSFER OF POWER

The 1946 elections demonstrated the potency of the Muslim League and showed that most of its strength was located in the Punjab, along the Indus and west of the river. Once the Muslims ended their support of foreign rule, the British position in India became untenable. As had been true a century earlier, the Indus was the basis for holding power on the subcontinent. With the Muslim-dominated Indus region no longer supporting them, the British responded by appointing Lord Louis Mountbatten as the last viceroy of India in 1947. Mountbatten, who was charged with overseeing "the transfer of power into Indian hands, decided to create a separate state for the Muslims."[35] Tentative agreements created what is now called Pakistan, but there was disagreement over three other territories: Bengal in the east and Punjab and Kashmir in the west. Indian and Pakistani leaders agreed to divide Bengal and Punjab, largely along religious lines. The two new countries could not agree on Kashmir, with Muslim leaders arguing for the Muslim-majority province. They eventually agreed to let Kashmir remain independent or join either country. After partition—the division of predominantly Muslim India (Pakistan) from predominantly Hindu India—the prince of Kashmir agreed to ally his region with India, resulting in armed conflict between Pakistan and India. Three separate wars (1948–1949, 1965–1966, 1971) failed to settle the issue. The question of who should rule in Kashmir remains heated and unresolved to this day.

Some view the British transfer of power in India as an example of good relations between a former colony and its former mother country. Others believe that separation was inevitable and Britain simply chose to swim with the tide rather than against it. Historian Paul Johnson, noting the region's extraordinary diversity, articulates the underlying conditions in his view:

> The reality is that the British government simply lost control. ∴ . . In 1945 India was over 400 million people: 250 million Hindus, 90 million Muslims, 6 million Sikhs, millions of sectarians, Buddhists, Christians; 500 independent princes and maharajahs; 23 main languages, 200 dialects; 3,000 castes, with 60 million untouchables at the bottom of the heap. . . .[36]

As Britain relinquished its control, some of these cultural and racial differences became important to India's inhabitants. Muslims wanted to live in a Muslim state, and Hindus wanted to live in a Hindu state. Once partition was agreed on, many emigrants traveled to either Hindu India or to Muslim Pakistan.

At midnight on August 14, 1947, India and Pakistan obtained their independence from Great Britain. In many respects, as far as the Indus was concerned, nothing changed.

The river continued its slow, purposeful flow to the Arabian Sea, as it had for millennia. Those living next to the river continued to rely on its waters for agricultural and drinking needs. For the first time in centuries, however, the vital Indus was not controlled by the largest power on the subcontinent. Politicians and leaders had altered the course of the river's history. In an instant, the river no longer was an "Indian" river. Instead, virtually the entire Indus River now belonged to Pakistan, the first modern nation created as an Islamic state.

7

The Indus Today

M odern Pakistan is one of the world's largest nations that predominately relies on a single river system. The Indus River and its tributaries supply about 60 percent of the water needed to meet the agricultural demands of more than 130 million people. In addition, dams and the production of electricity from the same system meet nearly half (45 percent) of the electricity need for Pakistan.

The river served as a water highway for much of its history, but its primary use changed under British rule as the colony became predominantly focused on agriculture. Other advancements, such as the construction of a railway through the Indus Valley in 1878 contributed to the decline of trade conducted on the river. With the growth of and dependence on the railroad, coupled with the expansion of the agricultural economy, the Indus began to play the familiar and increasingly important role of supplying water for irrigation. After India diverted three of the tributary rivers of the Indus (Ravi, Sutlej, and Beas) in 1948, Pakistan took steps to protect its irrigation system. The country began a canal construction program that allowed the diversion of water between rivers via canals. Today, so much water is removed from the Indus for irrigation that the river is used solely for small watercraft.

USING THE INDUS

Irrigation is the use of water from underground or surface sources. Underground sources require the lifting of water, and surface water is usually moved through canals. The Indus Valley is a semiarid plain that lacks sufficient rainfall to sustain agriculture. Because the valley is one of the most densely populated regions on Earth, irrigation is essential for the survival of the local residents and their cultures. Water can be made available to farmers in many different ways, including traditional methods and newer, more advanced technological means. These practices utilize ancient and modern technologies to draw water to the surface or exploit water already on the surface and include the Persian wheel, *karez*, tube wells, inundation irrigation, and canals.

The Persian wheel is one of the oldest means of bringing water to the surface; it works as a simple machine. An animal is harnessed to a shaft that is attached to a spur gear, which in turn is connected to another shaft that controls a bucket line. The buckets, powered by the beast of labor, are emptied into a ditch. Water from the ditch is then channeled to the field in need of water. Because of increased availability of gas and diesel-powered engines, the Persian wheel is disappearing from the region.

On the semiarid Indus Plain, the availability of groundwater decreases as one gets farther from the river. Because the Persian wheel is dependent on the accessibility of groundwater, other traditional methods for extracting water for irrigation exist. In the modern-day Pakistani province of Baluchistan, a traditional method called karez is still used for irrigation. Karez makes use of aquifers found in the foothills. These aquifers, supplied by melting snow, are usually small but are plentiful in the foothills. A horizontal tunnel is dug to link the aquifer to the village that needs water. The water is then released into an oasis or fountain that is easily accessible. These underground tunnels can be up to 12.5 miles long. In order to maintain the tunnel, vertical holes that link the surface with the horizontal tunnel are spaced about every 45 feet. Karez, then, is the system of underground channels and vertical shafts. The vertical maintenance shafts are needed to extract sand and other debris that collect in the tunnel. Without regular maintenance, the tunnels are eventually filled with sand and the water supply is lost. Karez agriculture is rapidly vanishing in Pakistan, in large part because of the use of tube wells.

Tube wells currently enable the most important source of groundwater irrigation in South Asia. Tube wells are simply metal tubes four to eight inches in diameter that are dug into the ground in order to reach the aquifers. Water is then pumped to the surface with electric or diesel engines. With this method, water is continually pumped to the surface. Because the government of Pakistan does not charge for electricity based on actual usage, many farmers have no incentive to conserve electricity. Instead, many tube-well owners simply allow the electric pump to continue drawing out water from the groundwater aquifer. The deeper the aquifer or the larger the tube's diameter, the more energy is required to pump the water—which increases production costs but not necessarily for the farmer. Since the 1960s, the number of farmers using tube-well technology has increased significantly. Profitability in food production, combined with advances in seed technology, has resulted in increased food production in South Asia.

In Pakistan, a primitive form of irrigation called inundation irrigation still exists. Inundation irrigation utilizes the annual flooding of the river, much like ancient Egyptians relied on the Nile for their irrigation and fertilizing needs. As the river rises, its overflow is fed into fields by special obstructions. These obstructions are made in advance of the flooding season. The rising floodwaters irrigate and replenish the soil.

Pakistani agriculturalists also make use of both small- and large-scale canals. Canals are made by constructing a dam and siphoning off a portion of the river. In small-scale canals, the dams might be simple structures made by river rocks. In these instances, the local residents manage the water flow by erecting and disassembling the temporary dam as needed. Large-scale canals are essential for irrigation and agricultural production in South Asia, especially in the Indus region of Pakistan. In large-scale canal irrigation, water is dammed and fed into a main canal. Next, it is routed into a main branch and then passes through two more levels (major and minor distributaries) before finally being siphoned off by individual landowners. The government of Pakistan is responsible for maintaining the dams and canals until the water reaches the last stage, which is made of watercourses that draw water from the minor distributaries and onto privately owned property.

Pakistani agriculture cannot survive without irrigation. Prior to 1967, Pakistan's canal system was unregulated and unpredictable. Farmers relied on consistent flow of the river, and so agricultural yield was significantly lower than it is now. The creation of dams and reservoirs helped conserve surplus waters of the monsoon season for use during the dry season. The irrigation system of the Indus basin is extensive: There are 3 major reservoirs, 16 barrages, 2 headworks, 2 siphons, 12 canals that interconnect rivers, 44 canal systems, and more than 107,000 watercourses. In addition, there are roughly one million miles of farm channels and field ditches. Pakistan's densely populated irrigated plain produces many agricultural products, especially wheat, corn, rice, millet, dates, and fruits.

Mismanagement of water resources still produces undesirable results. Canal irrigation without adequate drainage leads to water leakage, which in turn results in raised aquifers and waterlogged soil. In some of these areas, sunlight draws salt elements to the surface, producing soil high in salinity and negating many of the benefits of irrigation. These issues highlight the difficulty facing Pakistan because of its low annual rainfall: Pakistan needs to increase its managed or coordinated irrigation.

Because of the widespread use of the Indus for irrigation, the overall flow of the river has been reduced. As a consequence,

Construction on the Tarbela Dam in Pakistan was completed in 1977. The largest earth-filled dam in the world, standing 469 feet high and 8,997 feet wide, it is used to generate electricity for the country and provide water for irrigation of crops.

saltwater has crept up the river and caused damage to the surrounding countryside. The lower river in Sindh Province has lost "millions of acres of surrounding farmland to the sea or salt" as well as "hundreds of thousands of acres of ecologically important mangrove swamp."[37]

In addition to irrigation, the Indus provides hydroelectric power. The large Tarbela Dam, as well as a series of barrages

(continued on page 94)

THE INDUS RIVER DOLPHIN

Like many other large rivers of the world, the Indus River boasts a unique species: a freshwater dolphin, one of the rarest mammals on Earth. Other rivers that serve as home to various dolphin species include the Yangtze River in China, the Amazon and Orinoco Rivers in South America, and the Ganges, Brahmaputra, and Meghna river system in India, Bangladesh, and Nepal, respectively.[*] There are only four known river dolphin species, but the Indus River dolphin is found only in its namesake river—although it is closely related to the Ganges species. Until recently, the two were believed to be the same species, but marine biologists reclassified the Indus variety as a separate species because of its smaller size.

Local names for the Indus River dolphin include the Indus susu, the blind river dolphin, and the side-swimming dolphin. The Indus River dolphin

> has a long beak which thickens toward the tip, revealing the large teeth; the [mouth-line] curves upward. The body is stocky with a rounded belly, the flippers are large and paddle-shaped, and there is a low triangular hump in place of a "true" dorsal. The forehead is steep and the blowhole is on the left of the head, above the tiny, poorly-seeing eye. The tail flukes are broad in relation to the body size.[**]

The Indus River dolphin is gray-brown in color, sometimes with a pinkish belly, weighing up to 90 kg (200 pounds).[***]

The original habitat of the Indus dolphin included the entire Indus River, from the foothills of the Himalayas to the mouth of the river, as it flows into the Arabian Sea. The Indus dolphin primarily feeds on crustaceans such as prawns and fish such as gobi, catfish, and carp. The dolphin swims on its side and uses its snout and flipper to probe the bottom of the river in search of food.[†] Although the Indus dolphins prefer deeper water, they can survive in waters as shallow as three feet deep.[††]

The dolphin is often called "blind" because it is essentially sightless. This is probably because of the water in which it lives, which is so filled with silt that vision would be ineffectual. Because of these conditions, the dolphin's eyes have degenerated and it seems to rely on its sense of hearing and touch. The dolphin determines its location with respect to other animals or objects by emitting sound waves and sensing the pattern of the reflected sound waves, a process known as echolocation.

In order to breathe, the dolphin rises to the surface every 30 to 120 seconds. Occasionally, the dolphin exposes only the blowhole, but usually

The Indus dolphin once inhabited the entire Indus River but due to the construction of dams and barrages, its range has been significantly reduced. The Indus River dolphin is blind and uses echolocation—emitting sound waves and sensing the pattern of the reflected sound waves—to locate food in the murky waters of the river. This dolphin has been injured and is being cared for by Pakistani wildlife workers.

a good deal of the dolphin can be seen as it rises to the surface for each breath. Captive dolphins have been observed to swim continuously, perhaps because they spend their lives in the currents of the great river. The dolphins also make noises almost continuously, most of which are believed to be used for echolocation.

Until the recent construction of dams and barrages beginning in the 1930s, the Indus River dolphin was common and found throughout the

Indus River system in Pakistan, including in its major tributaries—the Chenab, Ravi, and Sutlej Rivers. The dolphin population would migrate downstream during the dry season and upstream during the monsoon season. The erection of dams and barrages divided the dolphin population into small groups, degraded habitat, and obstructed migration. Because the dams have isolated the dolphins into smaller groups, the resulting inbreeding has also hurt their numbers. In addition, the dolphins are sometimes hunted for meat, oil, and traditional medicinal purposes, and they are inadvertently entangled in fishing nets. Much of the remaining population is concentrated between the Sukkar and Guddu barrages in the Sindh Province of Pakistan.

Today, it is believed that fewer than 600 Indus River dolphins survive, although thanks to preservation efforts, the species' population is slightly increasing. Only the Baiji dolphin of the Yangtze River is more endangered. Although the animal is currently protected throughout its range on the Indus and is aided by environmental protection groups such as the Adventure Foundation Pakistan—a project funded by the United Nations—the Indus River dolphin is still classified as an endangered species.

* Adventure Pakistan Foundation. The Indus Dolphin: *http://indusdolphin.org.pk/about/*.
** Cetacea: Platanista minor: *http://www.cetacea.org/indus.htm*.
*** Animal Info—Indus River dolphin:
  http://www.animalinfo.org/species/cetacean/platmino.htm.
† Ibid.
†† The South Asian:
  http://www.the-south-asian.com/May2001/Blind%20Indus%20dolphins.htm.

(continued from page 91)

and headworks, provides electricity, water for irrigation, and flood control. The Tarbela Dam is the largest earth-filled dam in the world, rising at least 469 feet with a width of 8,997 feet. Construction began in 1968 and was completed in 1977 (it began operating the following year). It has a volume of 138.6 million cubic yards.[38]

Even with the extensive irrigation and its resulting lower annual flow, the Indus is still an impressive river. Its annual sediment discharge is the sixth largest in the world, and the area of its delta ranks seventh. Its annual runoff and drainage basin are the tenth and twelfth largest, respectively. At the delta shoreline, the wave power from the Indus entering the Arabian Sea is the fourth most powerful in the world. Its wave power ranks first in the distance the waves extend from the shoreline once the water depth reaches 10 meters (approximately 33 feet).

PROTECTING THE RIVER

India and Pakistan have argued over the use of the Indus and its tributaries since gaining their independence from Great Britain in 1947. In 1960, the two powers agreed to a treaty that dealt with the issue of use of the river and its primary tributaries (especially the Sutlej, which mostly flows through India). In 1991, the four provinces of Pakistan agreed to the Water Apportionment Accord, which divided and limited the amount of water to be used by each province.

THE FUTURE

What does the future hold for this mighty river of the Indian subcontinent? Perhaps its history can provide some clues. If the past is any indicator, the region will continue to be populated by individuals and communities that rely on it for survival. Like the many civilizations that have occupied land near the river, Pakistan today is a unique culture with its own distinctive traits. As different as Pakistan may be from the days of the Harappans, the Guptas, or the British, the country continues to exist because the river's water sustains the population's crops and industry, and will continue to in the years to come.

4000 B.C.	Evidence of management of rivers and flood plains in the Indus basin; use of bronze and copper.
3700 B.C.	First evidence of weaving at Mohenjo-daro.
3200 B.C.	Urbanization in northern India begins.
3000 B.C.	Beginning of Indus civilization.
2500–1500 B.C.	Indus Valley civilization flourishes at Harappa and Mohenjo-daro.
2300 B.C.	Trade between Indus civilization and Mesopotamian civilization; advanced city planning along the Indus; early scripts (seals) used.
1900 B.C.	Indus civilization begins to collapse.
1500 B.C.	Aryans arrive in northern India and the Indus Valley.

4000 B.C.
First management of rivers and flood plains in the Indus basin

3000 B.C.
Birth of Indus civilization

A.D. 1192
Muhammad of Ghur founds a Muslim empire in northern India

4000 B.C.   **A.D. 1000**   **1500**

327 B.C.
Alexander the Great invades India; Nearchus explores and maps the Indus

1900 B.C.
Indus civilization begins to collapse

1498
Vasco da Gama arrives in India

AFTER 1500 B.C.	Early forms of Hinduism are practiced; the Rig-Veda is composed in oral form.
c. 1000 B.C.	Use of iron begins.
900–400 B.C.	Later Vedas and Upanishads are written.
c. 563 B.C.	Buddha is born.
550 B.C.	Mahavira is born.
327 B.C.	Alexander the Great invades India; Nearchus explores and maps the Indus.
321–290S B.C.	Chandragupta Maurya's reign.
268–233 B.C.	Ashoka's reign.
262 B.C.	Ashoka converts to Buddhism.
2ND CENTURY A.D.	The Kushans, from Northwest China, extend their authority to northern portions of the Indus.

1885
The Indian National
Congress established

1991
Four Pakistani provinces sign the
Water Apportionment Accord

1850
British begin
construction of first
Indian railway

1977
Construction of
Tarbela Dam in
Pakistan completed

1600   1900   2000

1600
Queen Elizabeth I of
England charters the
East India Company

1947
India wins independence from Britain;
partition divides Muslim Pakistan,
including the Indus River, from
predominately Hindu India

1960
India and Pakistan
agree to share waters
of the Indus and
its tributaries

540   End of Gupta dynasty.

1192   Muhammad of Ghur founds a Muslim empire in northern India.

1498   Vasco da Gama arrives in India.

1526   Babur founds the Mogul Empire.

1556–1605   Reign of Akbar.

1600   Queen Elizabeth I of England charters the East India Company.

1757   Robert Clive wins Battle of Plassey; British become the dominant European power in India.

1840s   British forces in India take control of Sindh and Punjab Provinces.

1850   British begin construction of first Indian railway.

1857   Sepoy Mutiny begins.

1858   Control of India is transferred from East India Company to the British government.

1878   Construction of Indus Valley Railroad.

1885   Indian National Congress established.

1906   Muslim League founded.

1906–1908   Swedish explorer Sven Anders Hedin discovers the sources of the Indus and Brahmaputra Rivers in the Himalayas.

1919   Amritsar Massacre occurs; nearly 400 Indians killed by British.

1921   First meeting of the Indian parliament.

1947   India wins independence from Britain; partition divides Muslim Pakistan, including the Indus River, from predominately Hindu India.

1960   India and Pakistan agree to share waters of the Indus and its tributaries.

1977   Construction of Tarbela Dam in Pakistan completed.

1991   Four Pakistani provinces sign the Water Apportionment Accord.

NOTES

CHAPTER 1:
The Indus River and Valley

1 Gordon Johnson, *Cultural Atlas of India: India, Pakistan, Nepal, Bhutan, Bangladesh & Sri Lanka* (New York: Andromeda Oxford Limited, 1996), 13.

2 Ibid.

3 Ibid.

4 Ibid.

5 N.N. Bhattacharyya, *Ancient Indian History and Civilization: Trends and Perspectives* (Daryaganj, New Delhi, India: Manohar, 1988), x.

6 Johnson, *Cultural Atlas*, 13.

7 *http://www.travel-himalayas.com/rivers-himalayas/indus-river.html*.

8 Ibid.

9 Ibid.

10 Arrian, *Anabasis Alexandri and Indica*, trans., E. Iliff Robson (Cambridge, Mass.: Harvard University Press, 1966), 13.

11 Jane R. McIntosh, *A Peaceful Realm: The Rise and Fall of the Indus Civilization* (Cambridge, Mass.: Westview Press, 2002), 52.

12 Jonathan Mark Kenoyer, *Ancient Cities of the Indus Valley Civilization* (Oxford, U.K.: Oxford University Press, 1998), 29.

CHAPTER 2:
The Indus Valley Civilization

13 Burton Stein, *A History of India* (Malden, Mass.: Blackwell Publishers, 1998), 45.

14 Bhattacharyya, *Ancient Indian History*, 9.

15 Ibid., 10.

16 Ibid.

17 Ibid.

18 Ibid.

19 Ibid.

20 Johnson, *Cultural Atlas*, 19–20.

CHAPTER 3:
The Vedic Age

21 John P. McKay, et al., *A History of World Societies* (Boston, Mass.: Houghton Mifflin, 2004), 59.

22 Ibid., 61.

23 Bhattacharyya, *Ancient Indian History*, 145.

24 Arrian, *Anabasis Alexandri*, 13.

25 Alan Fildes and Joann Fletcher, *Alexander the Great: Son of the Gods* (Los Angeles, Calif.: The J. Paul Getty Museum, 2001), 119.

26 Richard E. Bohlander, *World Explorers and Discoverers* (New York: Da Capo Press, 1992), 319.

CHAPTER 4:
The Gupta Dynasty

27 Johnson, *Cultural Atlas*, 79.

28 Philip J. Adler, *World Civilizations* (Belmont, Calif.: Thomson/Wadsworth, 2003), 193.

29 McKay, et al., *World Societies*, 310–311.

30 Ibid., 312.

CHAPTER 5:
The Mogul Period

31 Johnson, *Cultural Atlas*, 85.

32 Ibid., 13.

33 Ibid.

CHAPTER 6:
British India

34 Kenoyer, *Ancient Cities*, 27.

35 J.P. Kenyon, *The Dictionary of British History* (Hertfordshire, U.K.: Markethouse Books, 1981), 187.

36 Paul Johnson, *Modern Times* (New York: HarperCollins Publishers, 1991), 469–474.

CHAPTER 7:
The Indus Today

37 *http://reference.allrefer.com/encyclopedia/I/Indus.html*.

38 *http://www.waterinfo.net.pk/fstd.htm*.

Adler, Philip J. *World Civilizations.* Belmont, Calif.: Thomson/ Wadsworth, 2003.

Arrian. *Anabasis Alexandri and Indica.* Cambridge, Mass.: Harvard University Press, 1966.

Auboyer, Jeannine. *Daily Life in Ancient India.* New York: The Macmillan Company, 1961.

Basham, A.L. *The Wonder That Was India.* New York: Taplinger Publishing Company, 1968.

Bhattacharyya, N.N. *Ancient Indian History and Civilization: Trends and Perspectives.* Daryaganj, New Delhi, India: Manohar, 1988.

Bohlander, Richard E., ed. *World Explorers and Discoverers.* New York: Da Capo Press, 1992.

Edwardes, Michael. *A History of India: From the Earliest Times to the Present Day.* New York: Farrar, Straus and Cudahy, 1961.

Embree, Ainslie T. *Sources of Indian Tradition.* Vols. 1–2, 2nd ed. New York: Columbia University Press, 1988.

Fildes, Alan, and Joann Fletcher. *Alexander the Great: Son of the Gods.* Los Angeles, Calif.: The J. Paul Getty Museum, 2001.

Griffiths, Sir Percival. *Modern India.* New York: Frederick A. Praeger, 1957.

Haywood, John. *Historical Atlas of the Classical World: 500 BC to AD 600.* New York: Barnes and Noble Books, 2002.

Johnson, Gordon. *Cultural Atlas of India: India, Pakistan, Nepal, Bhutan, Bangladesh & Sri Lanka.* New York: Andromeda Oxford Limited, 1996.

Johnson, Paul. *Modern Times.* New York: HarperCollins Publishers, 1991.

Keay, John. *India: A History.* New York: Atlantic Monthly Press, 2000.

Kenoyer, Jonathan Mark. *Ancient Cities of the Indus Valley Civilization.* Oxford, U.K.: Oxford University Press, 1998.

Kenyon, J.P. *The Dictionary of British History.* Ware, Hertfordshire, U.K.: Markethouse Books, 1981.

Lopez, Donald S. Jr., ed. *Religions of India in Practice*. Princeton, N.J.: Princeton University Press, 1995.

McIntosh, Jane R. *A Peaceful Realm: The Rise and Fall of the Indus Civilization*. Cambridge, Mass.: Westview Press, 2002.

McKay, John P., Bennett D. Hill, John Buckler, and Patricia Buckley Ebrey. *A History of World Societies*. Boston, Mass.: Houghton Mifflin, 2004.

Mitchell, Kate L. *India without Fable*. New York: Alfred E. Knopf, 1942.

Nehru, Jawaharlal. *The Discovery of India*. Garden City, N.Y.: Anchor Books, 1946.

Robb, Peter. *A History of India*. New York: Palgrave, 2002.

Sayeed, Khalid B. *Pakistan: The Formative Phase, 1857–1948*. London: Oxford University Press, 1968.

Scharfe, Hartmut. *The State in Indian Tradition*. Leiden, Netherlands: E.J. Brill, 1989.

Spear, Percival. *India: A Modern History*. Ann Arbor, Mich.: University of Michigan Press, 1961.

Stein, Burton. *A History of India*. Malden, Mass.: Blackwell Publishers, 1998.

Swan, Erin Pembrey. *India: Enchantment to the World*. New York: Children's Press, 2002.

Thapar, Romila. *A History of India*. Baltimore, Md.: Penguin Books, 1966.

Wilbur, Donald N. *Pakistan: Its People, Its Society, Its Culture*. New Haven, Conn.: Hraf Press, 1964.

Bryant, Edwin. *The Quest for the Origins of Vedic Culture: The Indo-Aryan Migration Debate.* Oxford, U.K.: Oxford University Press, 2001.

Fairley, Jean. *The Lion River, the Indus.* John Day Company. New York: 1975.

Kenoyer, Jonathan Mark. *Ancient Cities of the Indus Valley Civilization.* Oxford, U.K.: Oxford University Press, 1998.

McIntosh, Jane. *A Peaceful Realm: The Rise and Fall of the Indus Civilization.* Boulder, Colo.: Westview Press, 2001.

Watson, Jane. *The Indus, South Asia's Highway of History.* Champaign, Ill.: Garrard Publishing, 1970.

WEBSITES

Ancient Indus Valley Civilization
www.harappa.com/welcome.html

Harappa and Indus Civilization
http://www.wsu.edu/~dee/ANCINDIA/HARAPPA.HTM

Indus River
www.travel-himalayas.com/rivers-himalayas/indus-river.html

Indus River Dolphin
www.animalinfo.org/species/cetacean/platmino.htm

www.cetacea.org/indus.htm

http://indusdolphin.org.pk/about/

Indus River Facts
www.waterinfo.net.pk/fsib.htm

Indus Script
www.ancientscripts.com/indus.html

Indus (South Asian Physical Geography)
http://reference.allrefer.com/encyclopedia/I/Indus.html

WEBSITES *(continued)*

Rudyard Kipling
  www.nobel.se/literature/laureates/1907/kipling-bio.html

Tarbela Dam Facts
  www.waterinfo.net.pk/fstd.htm

Water Management in Pakistan
  www.riob.org/ag2000/pakistan.htm

SHANE MOUNTJOY is an Associate Professor of History at York College in York, Nebraska, where he resides with his wife, Vivian, and their four daughters. Professor Mountjoy teaches college level history, geography, and political science courses. He earned an Associate of Arts degree from York College, a Bachelor of Arts from Lubbock Christian University, a Master of Arts from the University of Nebraska-Lincoln, and a Ph.D. from the University of Missouri-Columbia. He is currently in his fifteenth year of teaching.

TIM McNEESE is an Associate Professor of History at York College in York, Nebraska, where he is currently in his thirteenth year of instruction. Professor McNeese earned an Associate of Arts degree from York College, a Bachelor of Arts in history and political science from Harding University, and a Master of Arts in history from Southwest Missouri State University.

A prolific author of books for elementary, middle and high school, and college readers, McNeese has published more than 70 books and educational materials over the past 20 years, on everything from Indian mythology to the building of the Great Wall of China. His writing has earned him a citation in the library reference work, "Something about the Author." His wife, Beverly, is an Assistant Professor of English at York College and the couple has two children, Noah and Summer. Readers are encouraged to contact Professor McNeese at tdmcneese@york.edu.